Enhancing Your Life at Home

TIPS FOR YOUR
Home Office

MEREDITH GOULD

A Storey Publishing Book

STOREY

Storey Communications, Inc.
Schoolhouse Road
Pownal, Vermont 05261

The mission of Storey Communications
is to serve our customers by publishing practical information
that encourages personal independence in harmony with the environment.

Edited by Pamela Lappies
Cover design by Mark Tomasi
Cover photograph by Eric Roth Photography
Text design by Jonathan Nix, Mark Tomasi
Production assistance by Susan Bernier and Erin Lincourt
Line drawings by Laura Tedeschi
Indexed by Word•a•bil•i•ty

Copyright © 1998 Meredith Gould

Printed in the United States by R.R. Donnelley
10 9 8 7 6 5 4 3 2 1

Library of Congress Cataloging-in-Publication Data

Gould, Meredith, 1951-
    Tips for your home office / Meredith Gould.
        p.   cm. — (Enhancing your life at home)
    "A Storey Publishing Book"
    ISBN 1-58017-003-X (pbk. : alk. paper)
    1. Home-based businesses. I. Title. II. Series.
HD2333.G68 1998
658'.041—dc21   97-35840
                                                                      CIP

CONTENTS

Dedication

For my parents, Bernie and Gerry Gould, both of whom in their own special way have made me constitutionally incapable of working in anyone else's office.

Acknowledgments

Thanks to the King of Networkers, Paul Block, for fixing me up with Pam Lappies. I am very proud to join legions of grateful writers in thanking Pam for being an editor who likes and respects writers. Thanks a heap to Storey Communications for letting me write in my own voice. And then there's my husband, Richard S. Ruch, about whom I could write volumes, plus Thelma and Louise, cat muses extraordinaire. Thanks, of course, to God for gracing my life with friends who do not hesitate to say "just keep writing" whenever I call them to whine.

Home Sweet Office

If you've picked this book off the shelf you're either working from home already, hoping to do so at some point, or an employer who understands the value of letting your employees telecommute from home. No matter what your circumstances, though, let me welcome you to the wild, woolly, occasionally worrisome, but generally wonderful world of working from home.

I stopped working from other people's offices in 1989, thanks to a strange opportunity I mustered the guts to pursue. We had just lost a major account at our small public relations company and since I was the vice president, I knew exactly how that loss would affect our quarterly numbers. It was, I figured, the perfect time to create one of those infamous, albeit elusive, win/win situations I'd read about in strategic management books.

There was nothing dreadfully wrong with where I worked. My co-workers were a small cadre of fun, talented folks and we were embedded within a larger ad agency that employed even more fun, talented folks to horse around with on a daily basis. I liked my boss, his boss, and a critical mass of other managers on the ad side.

I had my own office. It had not only a much-envied door, but also a big window with a glorious view of the woods. The kitchen, which sheltered continuous coffee, was right next door. On a bad day, my commute was maybe 20 minutes.

Nevertheless, I frequently found myself wondering why I had to go in every darn day. Almost all business was conducted by telephone, fax, and overnight mail delivery. Voice mail had just come into vogue, and the clients whose accounts I personally serviced preferred it to face-to-face meetings, a preference I heartily shared.

The only time I could do anything remotely creative was either before 8:30 in the morning or after 6:30 at night. There was simply too much hubbub during the workday. When I really wanted to get something done I stayed home — only I had to call in sick, because I had been taught that true professionals grind out work from their company holding tanks. Only lower occupational life forms like part-timers and amateurs worked from home. Eventually, I really did become sick, in addition to being sick and tired of an office grind not of my own making.

When we lost that big client, I made my boss an offer he couldn't refuse and have been working from home ever since — landing my own clients, paying my own health insurance, doing my own billing, and filing my own quarterly taxes.

Periodically, I still panic and think about going back Out There. Whenever that happens, I call one or two colleagues who work from home, then a few who don't. By the time I've finished those calls, I'm usually back to breathing normally and prayerfully grateful for my home office.

I won't say "I'll never" work in an outside office again — certainly stranger things have happened in my life. But it would have to be not only a pretty spectacular job opportunity, but also one that allowed me to: arrive in my jammies; eat lunch at 2:00; nap from 2:30 to 3:00; listen to Bach oratorios while preparing invoices; work out with my Ab Trainer (as seen on TV) while talking on the phone; sprawl on the floor when thinking up ideas; leave at 6:30 for dinner and *Entertainment Tonight,* then come back to work at 10:00 if I wanted. Of course I'd also have to be allowed to bring along my cats, Thelma and Louise, to snooze on my desk.

Would a conventional employer tolerate this wackiness? I seriously doubt it. Is it how I do my best and brightest work? You bet. And I know I am not alone.

As we approach the millennium, more and more people (double-digit millions, in fact) are rolling right out of bed and going directly to work in their homes. For quite a while now, both high and low technology have been available to transmit documents, close sales, research anything, transfer files, participate in conferences, play the stock market, move funds around, and review complex graphics without ever having to leave home. Today's wage-earners have a range of options. Some set up and manage their own businesses. Increasing numbers of employees maintain an on-site office presence most of the week and telecommute from home one or two days.

Home offices offer comforts, conveniences, and economic efficiencies that mesh well with today's work styles and lifestyles. Whether you're totally on your own or still an employee whose enlightened company management understands that working from home is equally likely to result in a job well done, you'll realize tremendous benefits from pursuing this work style.

You'll dramatically reduce commuting, wardrobe, and day-care expenses. Sooner rather than later you'll notice how working from home — even part-time — reduces psychological expenses as well. The emotional energy you've squandered on office politics and sucking up to your boss will become yours to use in more productive, effective, and creative ways. Like everyone else, you'll probably experience a sense of relief as you find and establish your own internal work flow. Time and space will acquire new meaning, as will organization and management.

But working at home does take some getting used to. Now that work and the rest of life are located in the same place, you'll need to develop a new set of disciplines. You may have to study up on codependency to learn about boundaries! You may have to join a support group to keep from snacking yourself into three hundred pounds! Some days you'll know, without a doubt, that E-mail needs to be tackled before laundry. Other days, doing laundry first will ensure continued sanity throughout the day.

If you're running your own full-time business, you'll be the one making decisions about everything — the look and feel of your actual work environment; the structure and flow of your workday; the equipment you simply must have to get the job done; how to convince clients and customers you're a player; and when to seek outside expertise. Now, if you hate your boss, you may have to invest in individual psychotherapy. You'll still need to make some of these decisions if you work from home part-time, but probably without the same financial pressure.

Here's the good news: You do not have to make everything up as you go along. Working from home is not uncharted territory, no matter how new it may seem to you. There's a much-better-than-average chance that the challenges, situations, or problems you'll face in your home office have already been faced by a community of others just like you. Isn't that a relief?

This book collects in one place tips and ideas that will not only help you get started, but also help you keep going strong. In the following chapters you'll find tips for enhancing your working-from-home experience. Some ideas will apply to your situation directly; others may need tweaking to fit your current — or projected — circumstances. And hang onto this book: You never know when you'll realize working from home is so for you that you'll quit your day job and go into business for yourself.

If these tips come as news, terrific. It's more likely, however, that they will remind you of things you once knew but forgot along the way. Perhaps you'll be inspired to try something you initially thought wouldn't work. Hopefully, this will be one book you'll happily refer to again and again as you become more at home with doing work from home.

1 Creating a Workable Environment

By the grace of God and whatever angels are in charge of real estate, my home office has always had a room of its own. This was true even when I rented New York City apartments — which, come to think of it, somehow managed to have great kitchens as well. But don't get me wrong: These fabulous separate offices weren't always set up in palatial extra bedrooms. One ended up in a dark, tunnel-like space so narrow that I'd slam into the opposite wall if I stood up from my desk too quickly. Another occupied a strange little sunroom-type area off the living room that, because it had windows on three sides, provided a fishbowl-like sensation. It was my 15th year of stacking all my books into the sturdy wooden pear crates I'd snagged during midnight runs to dumpsters behind fruit stands in Flushing, New York. I mention this only because I still remember the feeling of triumph that washed through me when I figured out how to stack the crates so that I had floor-to-windowsill bookcases. I quite frankly do not remember where I put my imposing bank of four-drawer file cabinets. I do know I jammed them into a closet when I moved to my next apartment — where, incidentally, I was able to stack the pear crates to create floor-to-ceiling bookcases. That office had hideous wall-to-wall shag carpeting that immediately camouflaged anything I was clumsy enough to drop off the edge of my desk.

Although my home offices have a track record for producing gasps of envy in covetous observers, I have to admit I'm kind of jealous of my mother's current setup. Walking into her Lilliputian one-bedroom co-op apartment, you'd never know what lurks behind closed doors. This woman, who specializes in successfully stuffing 10 pounds of you-know-what into any given 5-pound sack, has created a stunningly wonderful home office out of what could easily double as a linen closet. Open the door and out glides an entire office. It's magical and produces in me a ticklish mixture of pride and lust whenever I think about it. (You should see what she did with the bathroom–cum–art gallery.)

Truly there's part of me that wishes I could have the challenge of tucking an office underneath a stairway, or into a walk-in closet. What would I do if I had to carve office space out of a basement or attic? Would I indeed have the guts to ditch a dining room? While I'm grateful to have an extra bedroom to convert into office space, I wouldn't mind taking on the challenge of converting substandard space into something magnificently functional.

In this chapter I get my vicarious thrills by suggesting all sorts of space solutions for your home office, including how to create the illusion of space with color and lighting.

⊞ Even if you're squeezed for space, think twice — and then again — about setting up shop in your bedroom. Storing work-related equipment, materials, and even reading matter where you sleep will negatively affect the quality of your snooze time. If you must use your bedroom as an office, minimize the impact of this arrangement by:

• Keeping everything you need for work in only one section of the room.

• Creating visual and psychological separation by enclosing the area with a screen or other decorative barrier.

⊞ Convert a guest room to office space without sacrificing overnight accommodations by including a comfortable convertible couch on your list of essential office furnishings. Futons, whose frames don't have the bulk and heft of standard sofa beds, will allow you to save even more space.

⊞ Convert a closet into a mini work area by removing the door, cutting it down and installing it as a work surface, then replacing the clothing rods with shelves. If you already have an overhead closet light, terrific. Otherwise, a short strip of easy-to-install track lighting along the ceiling will do the trick. Install the necessary electrical outlets and don't forget about the sides of your closet space. Use them to hang things like T-squares or artwork only you can tolerate.

⊞ Closets are great places to stash file cabinets and still have storage space left over for supplies. Remember: Two-drawer file cabinets are more versatile than four-drawer cabinets.

⊞ Who says office furniture has to look a particular way? You can turn a funky wardrobe or an antique armoire into an office supplies cabinet, change a rustic trunk into extra storage space, and even create a conference area by using a coffee table with pull-out drawers, all with remarkably little effort.

⊞ Here are a few ways to create conference space:

- Configure your desk in a U-shape so that one section can be used as an impromptu conference table.

- Arrange your office so that your extra work surface — if you're blessed with the space to have one — is a freestanding table that can double as a conference table.

- Use the living room area of your home or apartment.

     Of course you could have an informal, unstated policy of never hosting meetings in your office. If you need to pull together a large group of people, consider teleconferencing the event. If you need to have a hunker-down work session with a group, consider renting meeting space at a local hotel, college, or conference center.

⊞ Stroll through your home with a new, critical eye for what can be transformed into storage space:

- Install shelving in your garage to store supplies that can weather any temperature.

- Perhaps there's a drawer or two in your existing dining room, living room, or bedroom furniture that could be put to better use for smaller, boxed supplies.

- Fill a sturdy, cardboard under-the-bed storage box with reams of paper and printer cartridges instead of clothes.

     Don't worry about having backup supplies out of immediate reach. In fact, it's probably better that they not clutter your work space. Just consider the hike to get them part of your exercise plan.

⊞ Whatever room or space you designate for office work will depend in large part on your work style and lifestyle preferences. Some issues to consider:

- Do you really want clients or visitors trooping through your house?

- Do you really want your family trooping through, or even past, your office?

- Are you primarily doing desk work? Do you need space to sort, store, and ship inventory? Are you producing and assembling a product?

- Do you want to keep your work-in-progress available and intact at all times?

- Are you easily distracted by noise, light, or activity?

⊞ Before you go through the effort and expense of rearranging electrical outlets, installing shelving, or buying office furniture, spend at least one full day in the area you hope to use as an office. No, you don't have to log an entire 8 to 10 hours at one sitting. You do have to be in there at enough key points during the day to discover whether you've truly found a workable environment. What seems perfectly quiet and well lit first thing in the morning may become dim and noisy by midafternoon. What works throughout the day might become intolerable once your entire family is in for the evening.

⊞ If you need to create two home offices but only have space for one:

- Choose the largest room available.

- Maximize privacy by arranging furniture into an L-shape, or any other way that keeps the two of you out of hearing range from one another.

- Use shelving, equipment, or furniture to create room dividers.

- Create a common area for shared equipment, resource material, and conversation.

- Develop a mutually satisfactory, agreed-upon-in-advance work schedule. Experiment with staggered office hours.

Note: This tip assumes that a spouse or intimate partner is involved. You may or may not want to create as much physical and psychological separation from someone you don't share the rest of your life with, such as a business partner or assistant.

▣ Want to carpet your office? Here are a few suggestions:

- Visit a few discount warehouse outlets where they sell broadloom remnants as well as carpeting by the yard. If they don't have commercial-quality floor coverings, look for a residential grade with short, tight, dense pile. Because you're looking at broadloom, you'll probably find a large enough piece at a lower price than you'd have to pay by the yard.

- Ask to see the whole piece. There shouldn't be any surprise defects, but you never know. Besides, you'll get a better sense of what the final result will look like when the entire remnant is unrolled on their floor before it gets to yours.

- Take whatever money you save by buying a broadloom remnant and invest it in higher-quality padding. You can actually get away with lower-grade carpet if the padding is rated "very good" or "excellent." Good padding also soaks up noise more effectively.

- Instead of having carpeting installed wall to wall, save money by having the edges bound on a remnant cut to the size of your room, or of the area you want carpeted.

- If you're installing new carpeting in your office, look for one that's commercial grade. Not only will its short nap wear better, but it will also create a visual and tactile demarcation between your office and the rest of your home. By the way, it doesn't have to be a dull and boring color — but do avoid choosing a pattern that's too jazzy or distinctive, because it may very well drive you batty over time.

- If you decide to go with carpeting (as opposed to hardwood, vinyl, or rubber tile), minimize static electricity by getting it specially treated. Humidifiers, plants, and antistatic mats will also help with this. (See also chapter 5.)

Feng shui (fung shway) is the ancient Asian art of arranging all the crap you want to stuff in your house so you don't freak out, go poor, drop dead, or get a headache from bad vibes.

For centuries, feng shui masters have been part of building teams throughout China and Japan. They are currently popular in the United States, especially but not exclusively among those who favor taking a more holistic approach to their home and work environments.

Since feng shui, which translated means "wind" and "water," is all about managing *chi* (energy), feng shui masters aim to correct whatever is causing energy to stagnate, leak, flow uncontrollably, or get all convoluted. They look at the placement of furniture relative to doors, windows, and other room openings. Color is important, as is the use of live objects such as plants and flowers. Feng shui masters are big on strategically placed aquariums, mirrors, crystals, and wind chimes.

Feng shui combines science, intuition, mysticism, astrology, sacred geometry, and common sense. If you've ever had a lousy night's sleep because you felt the bed was in the wrong position, you may have the wherewithal to dabble in feng shui. The basics include:

- Placing a live plant or aquarium in the "wealth corner" (farthest left corner of the room). If you get a fish tank, make sure you fill it with an odd number of fish. Apparently an even number will nullify whatever benefits the fish provide.
- Hanging mirrors high enough so your head (and chi) doesn't get chopped off.
- Suspending wind chimes before any door, especially at the end of a long, narrow corridor.
- Positioning seats so you face the door as it opens. Keeping seating against a wall provides support and stability.
- Hanging or placing plants in front of windows.
- Avoiding jagged, sharp edges or shapes that fracture energy.
- Crystals are considered the "aspirins" of feng shui — good for curing almost anything. Hang them wherever energy might escape; use them at the end of a long corridor to keep the energy moving.

Everyone says "Don't place your desk so your back is to the door," but I do. I've tried it the other way, but I'm infinitely more efficient when my back is to the door and my face is up against a wall. Maybe this is because I'm such a busybody that I cannot face an open door without being endlessly distracted, and closing it makes me too claustrophobic.

⊟ If your work area is already carpeted with residential-grade covering, there are other steps you can take to keep the space efficient. Try these:

- Put a sheet of stiff, heavy plastic underneath your desk. Not only will this protect the carpeting, but it will also enhance your mobility, since deeper pile will immobilize the casters on your desk chair.

- The next time you buy a desk chair, look for one with larger, three-inch casters — they work better on plusher surfaces.

⊟ Plan your home office decor to soak up as much sound as possible:

- Install acoustical ceiling tile.

- Surround the windows and doors with weather stripping.

- Treat yourself to a comfy, overstuffed chair or love seat.

- As I mentioned above, put the highest-grade padding you can afford under your carpeting.

- If floor-length draperies don't appeal to your aesthetic sense, decorate with textile sculptures or hang an antique quilt or rug on the wall.

- Cover one or more walls with cork, canvas, or special sound-absorbing fabric. These surfaces can double as bulletin boards.

- Replace the hollow-core door to your office with a solid-core one. (Don't forget to use the back of the door for a peg rack.)

⊞ An already enclosed balcony makes for cozy office space. Hang curtains or install an accordion-track room divider to separate it from the rest of the room.

⊞ Just because you have a formal dining room doesn't mean you have to use it that way. If your lifestyle is more casual, consider turning this into office space. Depending on the room's size, you may even be able to divide it into both a work area and a small conference area, or a room for an assistant. If at some point you suddenly feel like having a dinner party, plan to take your guests out to a nice restaurant. You'll end up saving money once you add the dollar value of your preparation and cleanup time to the cost of food and beverages.

⊞ Almost any room can be made to look larger with light colors, small patterns, and a few strategically placed mirrors.

⊞ Take another tour of your house, this time looking for nooks and crannies that can be converted into office space. Remember, all you really need is enough space for a work surface, your most essential desktop items, an electrical outlet, and a way to create decent lighting. With this in mind, look at the:

- Space underneath stairways.

- Breakfast room or nook off the kitchen.

- Landing or loft space between floors.

- Space at the end of hallways.

⊞ If you're prepared to do some renovations, possibly major ones, your options expand. Consider the:

• Attic.

• Basement.

• Deck off the living room or kitchen.

• Screened-in porch or sunroom.

• Breezeway between the house and garage.

• Carport.

• Garage.

⊞ If you have the resources, space, and wherewithal, you can build an:

• Entirely new, stand-alone structure in your backyard or adjacent to your house.

• Addition onto your house — perhaps a prefabricated structure such as a sunroom, or a second story.

As long as you're building, include a separate outside entrance if possible. This is especially important if your clients need privacy (for example, if you have a psychotherapy practice). Add a half-bath if you have the space and bucks.

⊞ If you suffer from seasonal affective disorder (i.e., you get gloomy, cranky, and sleepy during the darker winter months), install as many windows (and skylights) as your budget will allow.

⊞ If the best, most logical space available — like the basement — gives you the total creeps, keep scouting around for a work area.

⊞ Attic crawl space is perfect for storing dead files you rarely have to get into, or ones you cannot bear to toss even though they're duplicated elsewhere, such as:

- Clients from yesteryear.

- Clients who have gone out of business.

- Income tax returns.

- Diplomas, certificates, awards, commendations, plaques, and other stuff you think your kids (or biographers!) might want.

⊞ Cardboard file boxes are fine for storing documents in a dry place. Save the reinforced-steel safe for anything you want to keep fireproof.

⊞ Call your local engineering, architecture, or arts school before hiring an expensive architect or interior designer. These professional programs generally require students to design and complete a project for graduation. If time is not of the essence, you might find working with an enthusiastic, motivated student most rewarding. Contact the dean or department chair for information. If the school doesn't have such a requirement, ask for names of recent star graduates.

⊞ Need even more space?

- Install shelving or storage cabinets above doorways.

- Stack extra supplies underneath your desk, out of kicking range.

- Transfer as many paper files as you can to computer files. Get the reference materials you frequently use on CD-ROM.
    Note: Do this only if you're visually oriented (see the box on page 59). Otherwise, continue to let your fingers do the walking.

- Hang phones on the wall or on a stand mounted to the side of your desk.

You may not be able to physically expand your work space, but the right colors will make a huge difference. Color, well chosen, will fundamentally change the way you feel about your office and enhance your productivity while you're in it. The colors you choose will, of course, depend on what equipment and furnishings you already own, or plan to purchase. While there are general rules about mixing colors and textures, the best color scheme is the one that supports your productivity and creativity without whipping you into a psychological frenzy.

Remember, it's your home and your office. If you truly think you can deliver your product or service happily and on schedule from a purple office, go ahead and try. You can always repaint.

In general, keep these color characteristics in mind:
- Light, cool colors open up small rooms and raise ceilings.
- Dark, warm colors can make large rooms seem cozier and drop ceilings.
- Cool colors (blues, greens, grays) are calming.
- Warm colors (reds, yellows, oranges, browns) are stimulating.
- Complementary colors are energizing when used together.
- Bright, vivid, or dramatic colors (fire-engine red, egg-yolk yellow, milk-chocolate brown, black, purple) should be reserved for a few carefully chosen accent pieces.
- Sticking to a monochromatic color scheme (in which all the colors stay within the same family, just in different shades) is easier on the eye and brain.
- Adding white to any color to dilute its intensity results in a more calming, natural tone.

But there are a few anomalies:
- If you paint a small room in a very deep color, the corners will "disappear" and make the space seem larger.
- Even though they're different types of colors, efficiency is said to be enhanced by both grays and browns.
- All whites are not alike. You may find yourself feeling uncomfortable and even chilled if you use a white with blue tones.
- Depending on the quality of the available natural light, adobe-like colors (warm brown, burnt sienna) can actually cool down a room.

Also consider these facts:
- Color and lighting — natural and artificial — must be carefully coordinated. For example, to increase light you'll want to paint the walls opposite your windows a light color. If you are overwhelmed by light from windows or skylights, a dark color will soak it up like a visual sponge.
- Paint chips and swatches are simply not accurate indicators of how a color will look on a wall, let alone over an entire room. Buy the smallest amount of paint possible and paint part of a wall before committing to gallons. (It's easier to start light and go darker.)
- Woodwork, either wood furniture, as trim, or on walls or floor, should also be considered part of your color scheme:

Light woods	Maple, beech, pine, birch
Medium woods	Cherry, some mahogany, teak
Dark woods	Mahogany, dark cherry, walnut, ebony
Brown-toned woods	Walnut, dark cherry
Red-toned woods	Mahogany, maple
Yellow-toned woods	Teak, oak, beech

⊠ If storage space isn't an issue, divide larger rooms into different types of work space by using screens, accordion doors, plants, or drapes. If you always need more storage, use bookshelf dividers, file cabinets, wall units, or other pieces of multipurpose furniture.

⊠ Avoid building solid walls that extend from floor to ceiling unless you absolutely need privacy and your overall available space is large enough to override such visual density.

⊠ Stay as flexible as you can to allow for expansion, growth, and changing needs. In practical terms, this means resisting the urge to immediately bolt bookcases and office furniture onto the walls and floors, or build in desks and other work surfaces. Go as modular as possible.

⊠ Conversely, try not to make furniture rearranging your new, favorite work-avoidance strategy. You'll need time to see if you're meeting your work-flow needs. Try living with one arrangement for a fiscal quarter or two.

⊠ Wander through the housewares sections of discount retailers with an eye to using kitchen and laundry space savers in your office. Increase storage space by using:

• Undershelf baskets for in/out boxes.

• Flatware dividers for pens, pencils, etc.

• Wire pantry shelving for boxed supplies.

• Lazy Susans for frequently used desktop supplies.

• Wicker bread baskets for extension cords, AC adapters, telephone doodads, etc.

• Laundry baskets for supplies and recycling.

• Rattan hampers for large objects you want to keep out of sight.

▣ When storing supplies, group them according to function and task. For example, stash together everything necessary for mailings (envelopes, boxes, packing materials, stamps, labels); shelve printer cartridges with paper reams and so forth.

▣ Installing extra electrical outlets above the level of your desktop will spare you the hassle of belly-crawling along the floor whenever you need to plug in equipment you use regularly, but not every day.

▣ Narrow, "tower"-style bookcases will give you more placement flexibility than standard 36- or 48-inch-wide bookshelves without sacrificing space for books.

> **❝** I'm not big on having the office look so different from the rest of the house. I suppose some professions require it. I know a guy who's a lawyer at home. His office has lots of paneling. Very lawyerly. It kind of looks like a men's club and should probably be filled with cigar smoke.
>
> I'm in a creative business and my office, although it's entirely functional, is filled with childhood things that have meaning to me. Got to have those. Got to have fun and keep in touch with the old inner child. After all, he's the only one with the guts to write music. **❞**
>
> *Harry,* **film composer**

▣ Adding inside and outside corner bookcase units cuts down on wasted wall space and gives you a wall-to-wall library look. Some manufacturers make these in the narrower tower size.

▣ Consider stacking books, journals, and magazines horizontally as well as vertically on your bookshelves. This will provide both more space and visual relief.

▣ If you work from a wheelchair, you'll need to adjust desktop and cabinet heights accordingly. At least one manufacturer makes a line of pneumatically operated overhead storage cabinets.

⊞ All materials have subtle vibrational frequencies that will either enhance or reduce "visual noise," so pay attention as you pick out furnishings and accessories. Whether you use metal, wood, plastic, rattan, wicker, canvas, or some combination of these materials will make a difference in how you feel and perform in your work environment. If, for example, you need a slight boot in the butt to get going, then metal might provide a motivational edge. If you're already too hyper, consider furnishing your office in softer wood tones.

⊞ Unless you can afford to redecorate when you get bored, or know you need frequent changes to stay fresh, avoid:

• Trendy office decor (e.g., everything verdigris, art deco, or high-tech metal).

• Furnishings that show dirt, grease, and wear (e.g., matte black, unscrubbable surfaces, canvas fabrics).

⊞ If you need a change of office decor and don't have a lot of money to spend, focus on changing accessories and accents. If you have windowsill plants, buy a couple of standing ones. Change the color of all your desk tools. Install a screen saver on your computer. Use a mousepad that's a work of art. Don't just dream about plugging in your old lava lamp, do it.

If you can't get any work done while music is playing, it's probably because you're listening to the wrong kind. Certain combinations of sound and rhythm will lower your blood pressure, enhance your concentration, stimulate your creativity, and reverse your late-afternoon slump. Other music is guaranteed to jangle your nerves, reduce your focus, or make you cranky.

There's now enough research to suggest that this is one area where personal preference doesn't really matter. Classical music has proven to be far and away the most effective music to work by, but not all classical music works well. Here's a quick guide:

- The more measured, mathematical, and repetitious compositions of the baroque era (end of 16th century to early 18th century) will help you concentrate. Check out concerti and sonatas by: Bach, Vivaldi, Torelli, Telemann.
- The lighter, more buoyant works of the classical era (18th century) will help stimulate your creativity and productivity. Check out concerti, sonatas, and symphonies by: Mozart, Haydn.
- Except for Gregorian chant, which is unrelentingly repetitive, avoid vocal music — operas, cantatas, operettas, lieder, soft rock.
- Unless you spent your formative years in another culture and assimilated those rhythms and tones, stick to Western music.
- Avoid the plush, rhythmically complex, and colorful works of the romantic era (early and mid–19th century), the atonal weirdness of the 20th century, and most of the simplistic synthesized "New Age" music. While much of it is relaxing, it will do nothing to enhance your focus and productivity.
- Let purists cringe all they want, you can make auditory life easier on yourself by tuning in a good classical station (being sure to take a break if they start with the Shostakovich or Stravinsky). The Philips recording label offers classical collections custom mixed to support almost any environment or desired mood. Check out: *Mozart in the Morning, Mozart for Your Mind, Bach at Breakfast.*
- Save the rock, rap, jazz, movie tracks, and greatest hits albums for your cleaning or filing breaks.

It's already too noisy in my head, so why add music? Nevertheless, there are those times when I dose myself with Bach's *Brandenburg Concertos* or Vivaldi's *The Four Seasons* (on continuous play) to override the words and thoughts that are sloshing around in my brain. That's if I want to keep writing. If I really want to give myself a jolt, I play Vivaldi's *Gloria* at a zillion decibels and pretend to conduct it.

⊞ Dot the visual landscape of your office with objects, photographs, and artwork you find aesthetically pleasing, inspiring, or humorous. Some college or university libraries will actually lend art, as will artist friends who need storage space. Plan to rotate your personal gallery on a regular basis as a treat to yourself.

⊞ Listing everything you use every day will make it easier to determine what goes where. Observe yourself, noting which equipment, supplies, reference materials, and files you need readily available to function. Place these items within reach. Everything else should be stored elsewhere.

Now observe yourself again, this time noting the order and direction in which you do things. Use this information to arrange equipment according to your work sequence.

Good news for lefties: At long last you can truly have it your way.

" I like surrounding myself with very creative things and being able to move around the space. There's an angel that a friend sent me floating above my desk. Because I do kids' stuff, I have posters up on the walls. I like having my library of kids' books where I can see it and get inspired. My office is my domain, so I put things in there that make me feel good. **"**

Reba, **curriculum developer**

⊞ If you use the computer constantly and print out documents as fast as you generate them, these pieces of equipment belong on your primary work surface. If you use the computer only for select office functions, you can probably get away with stashing it in another part of the office.

⊞ When you buy lighting, match the type to the task. Ambient lighting, which lights up the room, should be uniform and moderately bright. Overhead lights, hanging fixtures, and floor lamps provide this kind of lighting. While you're at it, consider installing ceiling fans that come with lights.

> **❝** I don't bother with overhead lighting. I have it, but never turn it on because the rest of the equipment in here gets so hot that I don't want to add to the heat.
>
> "If I want to see anything I turn it on. If I need to see the computer, I turn it on. If I need to see the television, I turn it on. I have one powerful light over my desk, but don't even need to use that. **❞**
>
> *Thom,* **sound engineer**

⊞ Desk and table lamps, preferably with three-way bulbs, will provide light for detailed, intensive, or focused tasks.

⊞ Watch out for bouncing glares off computer monitors, furniture surfaces, windows, picture glass, or mirrors. Install dimmer switches to increase your lighting options.

⊞ Plug night-lights into a few electrical outlets or install motion-activated lights so you can dash into your office at night without having to turn everything on. Motion-activated lights are also handy if your arms are too full to reach for the switch.

AN EXPERT

- You have the space, you have the equipment, and you have the furnishings, but you're clueless as to how to put them all together in a way that's space-efficient and visually effective. Hire an interior designer by the hour. If you can find one with *feng shui* training, even better.

- You aren't exactly sure what you like and even if you were, you wouldn't know where to find it. You have no time to shop and wouldn't enjoy it even if you had the time. You long for someone who'd just listen to your wish list, show you samples, and make it all happen. Hire an interior decorator by the hour or job.

2 Equipping Yourself for Business

My father, then in his 70s, talked me into buying my first computer. I had been stubbornly clinging to my beloved IBM Selectric long after they stopped making the ribbon cartridges it needed. Dusting Kor-ecto-type flakes off the platen was an essential part of my work process. Another decade passed before I bought my own fax unit. I was very nervous about having to figure out the dedicated-line issue, but decided to resolve that after wasting a lot of time and money schlepping back and forth to the local public facsimile machine. Until recently, I somehow managed to survive without a Zip or tape drive backup system.

It's not that I was opposed to technology, it's just that it scared me. I suspect there's a hefty number of undisclosed technophobes out there, men and women who need to breathe deeply into little brown paper bags before buying anything requiring a power-surge protector.

I can cheerfully report that I've finally gotten over my fear of unknown and unseen things such as RAM, bytes, and defragging programs. I no longer believe I will be struck dead if I innocently place computer diskettes within a foot of my telephone during a thunderstorm two states away. I now rest in the comfort of knowing that whatever has disappeared from my computer monitor exists somewhere in the cyberworld, even if I am unable to find it.

While it may be possible to set up a home office without ultrasophisticated technology, you cannot operate a home office without a few key pieces of equipment — a desk, chair, and telephone spring immediately to my mind. The tips in this chapter focus on equipment basics. For the fancy stuff, you'll need to consult with a bona fide geek, a term I use with the utmost respect for anyone who can assemble anything without leaving a heap of screws and nuts abandoned on the floor.

1. A salesperson said I can't succeed without one.
2. Everyone else has one.
3. I want to be taken seriously.
4. It's on sale.
5. My brother-in-law, the expert, told me to get it.

⊠ Before rushing out to buy the latest and greatest office equipment, take some time to figure out if it would be more economical to use a local print or copy shop for some of your work. Really, how often will you need a desktop laminating system? A paper trimmer? A photocopier that makes double-sided copies, sorts, and staples 50 documents in three minutes?

⊠ When you prepare your budget for office equipment and furnishings, consider the following issues:

• Do you absolutely need to own this?

• Are there hidden costs to factor in, such as those for maintenance, supplies, accessories, special furniture, or storage?

• How will this purchase affect your efficiency, productivity, and income?

⊠ Invest in a good desk chair, one ergonomically suited to your body. Since this major investment ought to last a lifetime (okay, at least 20 years) it will be well worth your while to find an office furniture dealer who will let you try a chair on approval. What might feel terrific for 5 minutes in a showroom might not feel so great after a 10-hour day in your home office.

⊡ Adjustability is the key feature to look for in a desk chair. At minimum, you'll want the ability to adjust seat height. Remembering that the more options there are to tinker with, the more money you'll end up spending, check out chairs with:

- Back- and seat-tilt mechanisms that adjust for whatever weird, ergonomically incorrect postures you scrunch into. Both "posture-back" and "knee-tilt" mechanisms are designed to keep your feet on the ground even if you've tilted back to study the ceiling.

- Dual-wheel, self-locking casters that will allow you to roll around with the greatest of ease. Stationary chairs are fine if you don't mind staying in the same place and position all day long.

- Reclining options so you can lean back to relax without toppling over.

⊡ If you come in an unusual size — extra petite, pretty hefty, or extraordinarily tall — contact chair manufacturers directly. The top ones have designed products especially for people like you. In fact, having a chair custom made may ultimately end up saving you money once you calculate in what you'd probably spend on practitioners to heal your aching body.

⊡ Do you *need* armrests on your chair? Probably not. If you decide to get them, make sure they're short, support your forearms and elbows, slant down at the front, and are covered with a material that cushions without getting grungy (i.e., don't get ones covered with fabric).

⊟ Don't bother getting armrests if you:

- Are on a tight budget. Spend the money instead on a feature that's more important, like adjustability.
- Like to roll your chair right up under your desk or computer table.
- Find arm rests more distracting than relaxing.
- Like to sit cross-legged or fidget a lot.

⊟ Go ahead and get armrests if you:

- Are willing to pay extra for a little extra comfort.
- Have room for a wider and taller chair.

⊟ If you have space, invest in different types of work chairs:

- For general office work, buy a standard desk chair that you can adjust, roll across the floor, and get into and out of quickly without sprawling on the floor.
- For task-intensive work sessions that keep you glued to one place for quite a while, try a "kneeling" chair that stabilizes your back in its natural curvature.

⊟ Keep any paper files you're currently using within sight and reach. There are any number of products out there to keep them neatly organized, including ones that vertically stagger each file so they're easier to read. No room for desk trays on your desk surface? Install plastic wall pockets.

⊟ Get to know your computer and software by completing tutorial programs, reading the manual, or buying one of those popular guides for technophobes. If you can't or simply won't do this on your own, check out classes at your local community college. They probably have mini computer literacy courses for adult learners. (The ones for kids are probably too advanced!)

⊠ Superstores may be fun to wander through, but unless you're prepared to buy supplies in bulk, you may be better off buying individual items (e.g., staplers, tape dispensers, scissors) at regular office supply stores.

⊠ Unless you're extremely knowledgeable about the equipment you want or willing to do research in advance, stick with smaller stores for office furniture and computer accessories. The well-meaning clerks at superstores are rarely trained to do more than quote prices and lug boxes.

⊠ Can't stand shopping and schlepping? Order office supplies by phone, having everything shipped direct. You'll save time and money by buying in bulk through catalogs. But take time to study suppliers' delivery, credit, terms, and return policies before you order.

⊠ If you order by phone, prepare the form as if you were sending it. Recite your shopping list from it, then keep it to inventory what actually shows up at the front door.

Remember to ask if they offer a discount for on-line orders. If you don't need to talk with a real, live person, placing orders at odd times may be a time saver.

⊠ Each fiscal quarter, set up a specific date to buy office supplies in bulk. If you enjoy purchasing excursions, schedule them to coincide with quarterly taxes to offset the aggravation of dealing with your accountant.

⊠ Unless you're running a major business operation out of your home, you probably don't need a high-speed, super-volume, sorting and duplexing copier. Before talking with a salesperson about buying this equipment for your home office, know what your needs truly are:
• Are you only copying material that's 8½ by 11 inches? Or do you also need to copy legal- or ledger-size documents?

- How many copies will you need to make a month? If you're running up to a thousand copies, a personal copier is fine. Get a low-end machine if you're running only two thousand copies. *More* copies? Out of your home office? Really?

- Are the documents you copy brief ones? Or do they run on for dozens of pages that need sorting and stapling?

- How often do you need to reduce or enlarge whatever you're copying?

⊟ Before you buy any major equipment, ask:

- Other home-based businesspeople which brands they use and why.

- Local businesspeople how they rate their dealer's service.

- At least three different companies for bids that they provide after meeting with you in your office.

⊟ Try negotiating a deeper discount for cash purchases of equipment. Always remember to ask for a commercial discount.

⊟ Check with purchasing departments at local colleges or universities to find out what they do with used office equipment. Technical schools in particular upgrade to state-of-the-art equipment more frequently than you'd think. What doesn't get snapped up by faculty usually gets dumped or donated. You may be able to pick up surprisingly good stuff cheap.

HUMBLE **OPINION**

IN MY

Electronic equipment sure makes a difference in productivity, but my work life really turned around the day I bought a larger, deeper wastebasket.

⊠ As for equipment you're ready to unload, donate it to a school or other nonprofit organization. You get the tax deduction and they get something that has to be better than nothing.

⊠ Look for auction announcements in the newspaper. For example, FF&E ("Furniture, Fixtures, and Equipment") of the RTC (Resolution Trust Corporation) is this federal agency's division responsible for auctioning seized assets. But don't attend one of these wild events without doing your homework:

- Show up during their required inspection period to preview whatever is going on the auction block. Take careful notes, so that you can research the going market rate.

- On the big day, arrive with a budget and stop price firmly in mind, so you don't get swept away by your adrenal system — auctions proceed at a heart-pounding rate.

⊠ Some other great places to pick up good used office equipment and furniture include yard, moving, liquidation, and estate sales.

⊠ Purchase service agreements only for essential equipment. What's essential? Only *you* know if you can accomplish anything if a piece of equipment is on the fritz for a few hours, a whole day, or even an entire week. The service agreement should include:

- Regularly scheduled maintenance.

- Prompt response time to equipment emergencies.

- Information about which parts and labor are covered.

In addition, you can negotiate the inclusion of:

- Equipment loans if your equipment is out of commission for a while.

- A guaranteed response time of either two, four, or eight hours plus penalties if the repairperson is late or completely flakes out.

⊞ If space is at a premium, and perhaps even if it's not, consider buying a piece of multipurpose equipment, such as:

- A computer fax/modem.

- An integrated phone/answering machine/fax.

- A plain-paper copier/fax/scanner/printer.

Caution: What will happen to you and your business if this great piece of combination equipment goes on the blink? If you just felt a wave of nausea, forget about multipurpose equipment. If you feel relieved by the prospect of your office grinding to a halt, however, go ahead and check out these options.

LEASING EQUIPMENT

Buy equipment if you:
- Can afford to pay cash. Financing and leasing will increase the expense.
- Plan to own the equipment for quite a while.
- Want to keep your balance sheet clean of liabilities, and your credit lines open for other purchases.

Lease equipment if you:
- Need 100 percent financing.
- Expect to upgrade equipment quickly.
- Don't expect to cancel your lease before it's finished.

⊠ Check the monthly fee of voice mail against the one-time cost of an answering machine. Newer, more sophisticated answering machines will let you do almost everything a voice mail system will, including: remote calling in for messages, using security codes, leaving a voice memo for someone to pick up, creating different mailboxes, and providing callers with limitless blather-on time. You can even find one that, when you're away from your office, will call you to let you know you've received a message. And unlike voice mail systems, answering machines can pick up multiple lines and, most important, let you screen calls.

⊠ If you do a lot of international business, get a fax machine with "error correction," so documents transmit without losing speed even if there's noise on the line.

⊠ If you transmit artwork or photographs, spring the extra money for enhanced resolution settings and a plain-paper fax.

⊠ Stick to a stand-alone fax machine if you:

• Don't want to (or can't) leave your computer on all the time.

• Are a technological pygmy.

• Receive and transmit documents containing anything more elaborate than straight text.

• Always want or need hard copy.

> **"** State-of-the-art, sometimes referred to as 'bleeding edge', technology is usually a very costly capital expense. But that's peanuts when compared to the cost in time involved figuring out how to use it.
>
> Top-of-the-line is top-of-the-line until you walk out the door of the store you bought it from. With computers, especially, top-of-the-line is that for about a month — three, tops.
>
> I constantly juggle what I need now, what I will need in the future, and what I can afford. I advise new home office wannabes to watch their cash flow, then buy only as much as they can afford. **"**
>
> *Larry,* **industrial public relations writer**

⊠ Bring precise measurements, a blueprint, a floor plan, or your interior designer with you when you buy equipment. Don't forget to bring color swatches and carpet or fabric samples as well.

⊠ Long-distance service is so competitive these days that the major phone companies are always creating new packages for customers. But remember, they're in the business of selling services to you, so make a list of features you want and questions you have *before* coming under the thrall of customer service.

⊠ Remember the red "hot line" phone in the movies? You, too, can color- or style-code your phones:

- Choose different colors, then designate which phone is for personal calls and which is for business.

- Pick out equipment with different tones to help you figure out which one is ringing.

- Add at least one portable business phone to your equipment mix, although you might want to keep yet another phone handy in the kitchen or bathroom. If you get a top-quality phone with multiple secured channels, no one will ever guess you're on a cordless unit.

- Get at least one phone with caller ID, multiple lines, and a speaker-phone function.

- If you participate in a lot of conference calls, make sure one phone has three-way calling capabilities.

- Remember to get a phone with a mute button so you can tell your dog to shut up without clients hearing you go ballistic.

- Absolutely get a headset for the phone nearest (or on) your desk. Once you try one you'll wonder why you spent all those painful years tucking the receiver against your shoulder with your chin. Headsets are also available in cordless models.

⊠ No-brainer decisions: If you're faxing standard, business-size documents without detailed photos or graphics, and are not installing a dedicated line, you want:

- An automatic paper cutter.

- An automatic sheet feeder.

- A delayed sending feature, so you can transmit documents when phone rates are lower.

- Speed dialing and redialing.

- A fax/telephone switch.

⊠ At minimum you'll want two business lines. If you have enough clients to justify the cost, get a business calling plan that'll let you assign accounting codes for easier billing.

⊠ If you never want customers to get a busy signal and always want them to talk to a live human being, consider hiring a phone answering service.

⊠ Equip your home office with more than one fax machine if your business involves a high daily volume of faxes. As with any other piece of office equipment, sort out what you "must" have from what would be "nice to" have *before* shopping.

⊠ Other things to think about:

- Picking a fax machine that doesn't require a dedicated line.

- Expanding your capacity for incoming calls by adding a phone number with a special identifying ring and call waiting. Many people despise call waiting, but don't let that stop you from getting it. You can disable it before making a call that cannot be interrupted, ignore it and let the caller call back, or simply say, "I'm being beeped, may I put you on hold for a minute?"

⊠ Make a note in your calendar to re-research phone systems every quarter so you don't miss any money-saving options.

⊠ There are zillions of very tempting, seemingly handy items out there. What you need to remember is this: One person's necessity is another person's gadget — and vice versa. Knowing whether you respond better to visual, auditory, or kinesthetic cues will help you decide if a piece of equipment or software is really going to work for you.

For example, if you need to touch something other than buttons to believe anything is actually being accomplished, you may be driven stark raving mad by electronic desk organizers, dictation recorders, and any software that allows you to do everything on-line. (See also the box on page 59.)

As for acquiring these gizmos, your best bet is buying them from stores, dealers, or mail-order catalogs with generous, reliable refund policies.

⊠ Don't wait too long for the magical moment of complete satisfaction to occur. If you don't like the feel, sight, or sound of whatever you bought within a week or so, you probably never will. Return rejects promptly.

> **"** Most computer magazines have lists of the "best" shareware, or shareware of the month. See if you can find reviews of a particular shareware you're interested in, then wait about three months from the time you read the review, because there might be a letter to the editor about it that will influence your decision. **"**
>
> *Larry,* **industrial public relations writer**

⊠ Downloading shareware written by members of the Association of Shareware Professionals is a good way to try out reputable computer software.

⊠ Get as much office equipment as possible off the floor, onto rolling casters, mounted to the walls, hung from the ceiling, close to electrical outlets, away from heat registers, and nowhere near small children.

⊠ Protect equipment and save utility costs by installing separate zone temperature controls for your home office.

⊠ Protect equipment from burglary by installing a security system. Depending upon how much expensive stuff you have and where it's located, a basic motion detector might do. Obviously, if you have a million bucks' worth of recording equipment in your back bedroom, spring for a more comprehensive, hard wired system.

⊠ If you work with private, confidential material, install a security lock on your office door and buy filing cabinets with locks. Then use them.

⊠ Add smoke detectors and fire extinguishers to your equipment shopping list.

⊠ If you read computer magazines, talk with friends, or consult with any one of today's teens, brace yourself for a plethora of well-meaning and occasionally well-educated opinions about what they think you should buy. Here, basically, is what you need to consider:

• Mac or MS-DOS? Rarely will you find anyone who is equally passionate about both. Quite frankly, it's all a matter of personal preference. Unless there's an industry standard that's different from what you're used to, go with whichever system you know best.

- What's it primarily being used for? Word processing only? Word processing and some spreadsheet work? Accounting programs? Desktop publishing? Searching through CD-ROMs? Make a list of all the office functions you want computerized. This will determine how fast a processor (how many MHz) to get.

- What software comes with it? What software do you want to use? This will determine how much hard-drive memory (MB of RAM) to get.

- How upgradeable is the equipment? Will you be able to attach an ergonomic keyboard? Replace the mouse with a track-ball?

- How portable is the equipment and how portable do you need it to be? This will determine whether to get a desktop system, notebook, handheld model, or some combination with a docking station for connectivity.

- Will you need technical support? How much?

▣ Save brain cells and preserve your sanity by making a realistic list of computer features you need (versus what would be nice to have) *before* starting your research, let alone the actual shopping.

▣ No-brainer decisions: If you're doing basic word processing, running an accounting program, and using e-mail, you want:

- An internal modem of at least 28,800 baud.

- A 3½-inch drive that accommodates a 1.44 MB diskette.

- A 14-inch monochrome monitor with SuperVGA resolution — unless you're highly visual and easily bored, in which case buy a color monitor. Obviously, spring for color if you plan to tinker with graphics. (Be sure to buy the monitor separately. The ones that come with package deals usually aren't the greatest.)

- A surge protector and a source of backup power.

- A backup, portable hard drive or disk drive.

- A warranty that runs for a full year or longer. Remember, you can usually extend your warranty automatically by using one of the major credit cards.

⊠ While you're at it, buy at least one inkjet or laser printer. They're affordable and quiet. Buy a workhorse of a model that has a documented reputation for churning out thousands of pages a month without breaking down.

⊠ The standard height for writing desks is 30 inches; for computer desks it's 26 inches. For a 14- to 15-inch monitor, you'll need at least 16 inches of depth, plus another 3 to 6 inches for wires and cables.

⊠ If you have the space:

- Get a desk that's deep enough for your computer yet still provides space for writing; wide enough to hold essential equipment within reach and without crowding.

- Supplement your traditional sit-down desk with a standing work surface. Standing reduces spinal stress by 50 percent.

- Configure your desk in an L- or U-shape to provide more work surface and conference space.

> **"** I buy all my office equipment — especially computers and computer products — via mail order. Retail outlets have notoriously poor service, and I generally would not want to entrust my technological wonder to their service departments.
>
> Modern equipment is not like an old car. Rarely can it be tinkered with. I'd rather find a company with a lengthy warranty and a reputation for service and send back my equipment if something goes wrong. Not only will the service be done correctly, it will usually be done far more quickly. Furthermore, the mail-order cost savings can be extremely significant, especially when factoring in sales tax savings. For the price of a middle-of-the-line item at a retail outlet, you may be able to buy via mail order that state-of-the-art model you really want. **"**
>
> *Paul,* **novelist and editor**

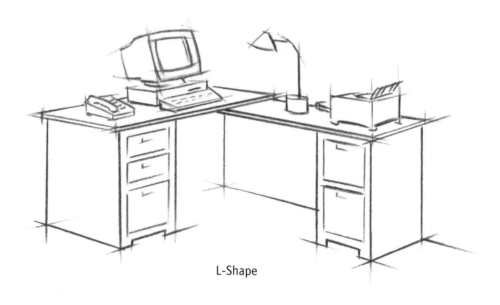

L-Shape

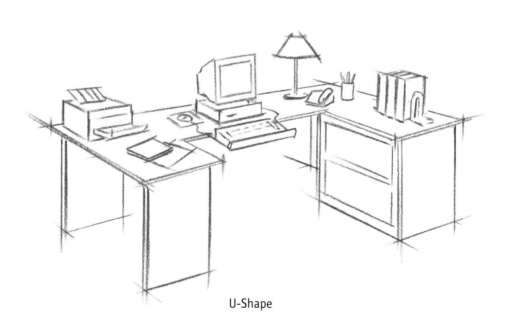

U-Shape

⊠ If you don't have the room to add an L to your desk, use the surface of a rolling two-drawer cabinet. Find one that has a top drawer in which you can keep office supplies and a bottom drawer for active files.

⊠ Beware of great deals, "refurbished" equipment, switched parts, anything that doesn't come in a factory-sealed manufacturers' box, and being talked into anything more, bigger, or allegedly better than what you initially decided to buy.

⊠ Create recycling bins by using laundry baskets or step-on cans that you label or color-code. Make schlepping this stuff out of your office easier by lining whatever you're using for cans and bottles with a sturdy plastic garbage bag.

⊠ You can easily make the most practical, least expensive desk on the planet by stacking a 26 x 68-inch door on a couple of two-drawer file cabinets, sawhorses, or anything else that makes it possible for you to sit comfortably without scraping your thighs.

- You have a history of lower back problems plus shoulder injuries. You blew out your knees back in undergraduate school and your elbows aren't in such great shape nowadays. Find a personal trainer, physical therapist, or therapeutic bodyworker who can evaluate your physical comfort in relation to your office equipment and how it is situated in the office environment. If possible, have this person accompany you to office equipment showrooms.

- You've invested in state-of-the-art software, have read and reread all the supporting materials, but still suspect you're losing precious time (and brain cells) trying to figure it out. Have someone who is computer-proficient come in to give you a private tutorial in front of your computer in your office. Remember to find someone who is able to teach. For your purposes, technical proficiency is virtually worthless without communication skills.

- You're about ready to hang yourself by a telephone cord because the range of options in equipment and services is making you nuts. The phone companies offer free advice about the service they're selling, but you may be better off working with an independent consultant who can come see your situation and spend a chunk of time with you.

- You suspect that your fabulous 21st-century office equipment might not work with your 20th-century wiring system. Get everything checked by an electrical contractor before plugging anything into the wall sockets.

3

Designing a Work Flow That Works

Go ahead and skip through your home shouting, "Free at last, free at last, thank God Almighty, free at last," but don't get too carried away. There's work to do and now that you're fully in charge, you'll have to figure out how to get it done efficiently and effectively. Do you absolutely need to handle routine assignments on weekends? Will eating lunch at your desk really give you more time? Is making business calls from your car safe?

True confession: I've been on my own for years and I'm still working out the kinks that gnarl my work flow whenever circumstances, clients, or projects change. Some of the systems I figured out early on have remained constant, such as my super-duper junk mail jettison routine. Others, such as how I batch errands and code projects, have changed over time and will change again. I'm a keen advocate of having enough constancy to provide a sense of security, and enough change to keep it all interesting.

You, of course, will find your own balance, which in turn will depend on your particular circumstances as well as your learning style. Let me suggest that you'll save yourself oodles of grief if you figure out how you perceive and organize information before cooking up any snazzy work-flow systems. In fact, I invite you to flip ahead in this chapter to where the three learning styles are described (page 59). Study them first and keep them in mind as you forge ahead, choose equipment, and create a workable environment.

Next topic: Kids. I don't have any around, but some of my best friends do. From speaking with them, lurking around the Working from Home Forum on Compuserve, and interacting with colleagues, clients, and vendors, I've come to believe that there has been a slight shift in tolerance for this home-based work circumstance. While I doubt baby wails will ever be considered an appropriate ambience for conference calls, I do believe there's an increasing number of family-friendly folks out there. I'm not so sure that blowing your cover about having a home office as well as kids at home will deal a fatal blow to your business. Call me crazy, but I'm beginning to think that businesspeople actually like to know that there are humans among us.

As with everything else, designing a work flow that works with children in the mix takes a certain level of discernment, creativity, and appreciation for the realities of business. I am awed by those of you who gracefully manage this juggling act. Some days it's all I can do to get any work done with the cats clamoring for food in between their naps.

⊟ Create a routine to distinguish your morning-at-home from your morning-at-work. Try leaving the house for early errands or exercise, then coming back and going directly to your office. Experiment with starting your workday by watching a morning news show, or reading a newspaper.

⊟ Once at your desk, try reviewing your calendar and "To Do" list, then immediately return important calls to get into the work groove. If these work-related tasks don't get you going, you may just have to get fully dressed in corporate-like duds. Sorry.

⊟ If at all feasible, designate one door of your home for business and another for family traffic. To further separate work from family life, leave for work from the family door and reenter your office through the business door each morning, reversing the process each night. This may seem like a hassle, but the psychological benefits of this maneuver are enormous.

HUMBLE
OPINION

IN MY

Dressing up for work at home is highly overrated. I didn't leave a traditional office to jam myself into pantyhose every day. Gee whiz, even corporations have adopted a dress code called "business casual."

The only time I dress up to sit at my desk in the privacy of my home office is when I'm trying to collect money from the artful dodgers in accounts payable. Sometimes, if I'm making my third round of calls, I'll put on something with shoulder pads. Otherwise, my home version of business casual is a hooded sweatshirt tastefully layered over a flannel nightgown, in the winter. For summer, I switch to a sports bra and bib overall shorts.

I make every effort to shower and change into real clothes before my husband comes home, to keep up appearances.

> **"** My transition ritual? Get the hell out of bed!
>
> Some of my customers don't even get in until 9:00 in the morning, others at 7:30. If you want to keep food on the table, you do what you have to to be motivated. Depending on who I'm trying to catch, I do what I need to do, when I need to do it. That's one of the freedoms of being in sales and not in an office.
>
> I go with the flow and have to be very self-motivated, but I like that. I've had the other extreme of having to punch a clock and this is much better. **"**
>
> *Karyn,* **medical equipment sales**

⊞ If your business doesn't rely on standard office hours, experiment with a variety of schedules to discover your optimal working time.

⊞ Pick any schedule to follow for a week or two, keeping a daily time log of your productivity. You'll want to track what you did, when you did it, and how long each task took. After trying at least three different configurations, compare schedules to discover which hours you were most productive, then establish your regular work schedule accordingly.

⊞ Make meetings — either on the telephone or in person — more efficient by scheduling appointments at unusual times. You'll project an impression of limited time availability if you schedule a meeting for 9:40 A.M. rather than at 9:00 or 9:30. If you're prepared to hunker down for a work session that might span a few hours, go ahead and schedule that meeting on the hour or half-hour.

⊞ Unless you conduct bicoastal or international business, make every effort to limit your business telephone usage to standard business hours. Even if your creative juices flow more freely on the night shift, keep a few "normal" working hours available. If you're a night owl, put electronic mail and voice mail on your gratitude list, because they can be used at any bizarre hour.

⊠ If you don't usually wake up before noon, let your answering machine pick up the call. Why risk sounding sleepy, incoherent, and unprofessional?

⊠ Before establishing regular office hours, you'll need to:

• Define what a "good day's work" is for you.

• Determine how many hours you'll need to accomplish your goals.

• Find out what are considered standard office hours in your business or industry.

⊠ Don't be surprised if you find that the number of hours you *need* to work exceeds the number of hours you *want* to work. This is especially true at the start-up of a business, or when major projects loom on the horizon.

⊠ Learn to distinguish urgency from importance by asking yourself these questions:

• What is the worst that could happen if I didn't do this now?

• Is this the best use of my time right now?

• What would happen (to me, my career, my life) if this never got done?

⊠ Know thyself! If you need to ease into the day's work, get started by doing the easiest, most exciting, most interesting item on your "To Do" list. If you revel in accomplishment, get the toughest, most odious task out of the way first thing.

⊠ You'll get much more accomplished to completion if you designate specific times to turn off the telephone ringer and resist checking for messages during your concentrated work time.

⊠ Increase your chances of catching senior management people by calling right before, or just after, regular working hours. Secretaries, assistants, and other gatekeepers are generally not around at these times. You'll also increase the likelihood of contacting these folks if you note what time your calls get returned by them and call back at those times.

Incidentally, voice mail actually seems to increase the likelihood of direct contact if you know the direct extension. If you don't, stay on the line until you hear all the menu selections, since most systems include some sort of directory option.

⊠ Plan for unexpected calls and garden-variety distractions. How? By leaving room in your daily schedule for last-minute opportunities and hassles. These will always come up and you won't get behind if you've already set aside the time.

⊠ Save routine, no-brainer tasks like filing, cleaning, and errands for when you are least able to concentrate. More often than not, if you distract your mind and occupy your body with this necessary junk, you'll come back to work refreshed, reinspired, and ready to concentrate.

⊞ Batch phone calls and return them in one fell swoop when you need a break from other kinds of work. Schedule this activity as the transition from no-brainer work to kicking into high gear.

⊞ Create a "milk route" for errands and make it a regular part of your routine. Think through the most efficient way to group the tasks you need to accomplish before even stepping out of your office. Batch errands by location, then map out a route so you loop around rather than backtrack to get home.

⊞ If you haven't done this already, choose a dry cleaner, supermarket, pharmacy, bank, gas station, mailing service, and video store in the same shopping center.

⊞ Carefully examine your list to see if there's anything you can do more easily by phone, like banking, bill paying, or ordering supplies. On the other hand, you may need to take a drive, but be sure to notice which errands waste time instead of restoring energy. (Hint: If you schedule errands during traffic-heavy hours you're practically guaranteed to feel drained.)

HUMBLE OPINION

IN MY

Doing housework is part of my creative process. Quite frankly, I like making it an efficiency exercise as well. Why not toss in a load of laundry while waiting for a document to print out? I've had major creative epiphanies while vacuuming. I suspect that most people with home offices do as well, and that denying ourselves access to the available flexibility of having an office at home is hubris, insanity, or both.

⊠ Write out your errand route, rather than trying to commit it to memory. If you sequentially number each stop, you'll greatly increase chances of getting everything done. And don't forget to indulge in the ultimate satisfaction of crossing tasks off your list as you complete them.

⊠ Taking time to determine what, for you, is a waste of time is time well spent. The business benefits you receive from attending that monthly luncheon with people in your field may more than compensate for the time spent attending. Making a phone call may be more efficient than writing a letter, but if you're a writer, this activity may be precisely the warm-up you need. Taking mail to the post office or mail service wastes time only if you don't do anything else along the way. It's absolutely not a waste of time if the postmaster is the first living, breathing human being you've talked to in days.

⊠ Beware of taking on someone else's definition of a time waster. It may be precisely the activity that keeps you balanced and sane.

⊠ Stay current in your field by saving newsletters and clipping pertinent articles from magazines as you see them. Stash everything in a file to read while stuck in traffic, standing in lines, or sitting in waiting rooms.

> " Very little distracts me and I think a lot of people are downright awed by my ability to go down to the basement and work. At 5:30 almost every morning, I grab my carafe of coffee and commute downstairs. I close the door and I'm away from home. I easily put in 12 hours of work a day, sometimes more. If at any time I feel like I'm losing my focus, I open my file drawer and look at my mortgage note or my daughter's tuition bill. "
>
> *Stuart,* **market researcher**

⊠ Pass along articles you've finished reading to contacts you want to cultivate and colleagues you want to maintain. You cannot overestimate the positive impact of receiving a clipping with a short, thoughtful "FYI" note attached. And do not limit yourself to sending purely business-related tomes. Forwarding cartoons, health care information, easy recipes, child-rearing hints, and pet tips lets people know you're paying attention to not only what they do, but also who they are.

Done with an article? Toss it immediately or pass it along unless it:

- Contains generic information not readily available elsewhere.

- Inspires you to try something new and different.

- Makes you laugh out loud.

- Mentions you. You know, of course, not only to keep this, but also to make lots of copies to pass along.

⊠ Unless you specialize in writing direct-mail copy, don't even open junk mail. If you're a copywriter, save the best for your "swipe" file. Otherwise, head directly for the recycling bins you've strategically placed between mailbox and office. Do not go anywhere near your office with this stuff.

⊞ Go to the other person's office if you:

- Can do other errands on the way.

- Do not have a lot of time to schmooze and want to control the meeting time.

- Need some outside stimulation.

- Want to be dressed like a grown-up where someone can see it.

- Don't feel like cleaning your office for public viewing.

- Have pets that growl, bark, drool, or shed profusely.

- Have sick kids at home.

⊞ Let them come to your office if you:

- Have materials or equipment that cannot be transported.

- Cannot spare the travel time.

⊞ You cannot have too many clocks, especially if you tend to space out. Mount a clock on your office wall, put a clock on your desk, keep one on your bookshelf. Use alarm clocks for stress breaks and timed activities. Do business in another time zone? Keep a clock set accordingly so you don't make ill-timed phone calls.

⊞ Get clocks that are numeric as well as digital. Look for a beautiful, antique hourglass. Go designer, classic, or artsy. Treat yourself to a timepiece that's so silly you grin every time you look at it.

> **"** Voice mail has made my professional life much easier because I can sit at my desk, fire off a list of questions in my own words, then move on to something else. I may end up playing telephone tag more often, but even that seems quicker. If I don't hear back, I just leave another message saying something like, 'I really need to hear from you today.' **"**
>
> *Jan,* **art reviewer**

⊠ If you really intend to work during a business lunch, here are some suggestions:

• Pick a place where that can actually happen. The eatery should have tables large enough to accommodate materials or a notebook computer. Ask for a corner booth.

• You want the meal to be decent, but not so overwhelming that it makes working impossible. Save fancy food for celebrations. If there's alcohol available, make sure it's not going into *your* bloodstream. Concentrating at a business meal is tough enough without booze-induced fuzziness.

• As for timing, schedule business lunches either right before or right after prime mealtimes, to receive better service.

• And don't forget: Tip more than 20 percent if you've tied up the table for over two hours.

⊠ You're the secretary now, so:

• Pencil filing and response notes directly onto memos and letters as you read.

• Note phone call details directly on whatever you're responding to: date and time of the call; name of the person you spoke with; follow-up required on your part; action they've agreed to take; and deadlines.

> **"** When I go into the field I get dressed up, but in my office at home I prefer to be comfortable. It doesn't affect my professionalism. When I talk to people it's serious — I'm trying to give information, get information, or get an appointment. It's just the same as if I were out there in a suit, face to face.
>
> People buy from people they're comfortable with. You have to have comfort within your professionalism to be successful. **"**
>
> *Wendy,* **media buyer**

- Immediately dump whatever does not need filing or follow-up. (If you have a cat, crumple this stuff up into a ball and toss it across the room.)

⊠ Calendar tricks:

- Match the format to the scope of activities, using month-at-a-glance for big events, week-at-a-glance for appointments, and day-at-a-glance for "To Do" lists.

- Even if your preferred calendar system doesn't include this feature, write your major goal for each week at the top of that week's page.

- Each January: Mark all important birthdays, standing appointments, anniversaries, business conferences, school events, payment deadlines, and general holidays for the upcoming year.

- Keep a calendar where you are most likely to make dates and appointments — by the phone, in your briefcase or your purse.

- If you keep more than one calendar, be extra-sure to copy dates from one to another on a regular basis. Set up a specific time to do this each week.

- When you get invited to something you actually plan to attend, put the date as well as directions in your calendar. (Be sure to RSVP immediately. Your courtesy will be greatly appreciated.)

⊠ Don't be so quick to de-clutter your desk just because practically every efficiency expert suggests doing so. Neatness and organization are not necessarily the same thing. If you're visual, you may need to keep active projects in your sight line. If you're kinesthetic, the physical act of shuffling papers may be exactly what you need to get started.

⊞ There's no shortage of cleverly conceived mail-sorting systems, but they all contain the same basic components, so don't get too hung up on any particular system. Ultimately, you'll need to do one of the following with whatever lands on your desk:

- Act immediately.

- File for future reference.

- Read at leisure.

- Trash.

⊞ You can easily extend these principles to sorting electronic mail by immediately:

- Using the "reply" command to respond.

- Transferring the keepers to the "filing cabinet."

- Hitting "delete" with delight and gusto.

⊞ Many of the rules you develop for filing can be applied to e-mail as well, but also remember to:

- Configure your software to automatically save and file mail you send.

- Consolidate outgoing mail and replies into one "thread" document.

- Transfer e-mail you want to keep onto a floppy disk.

- Use last *and* first names of people on your file folders.

⊞ Sort items to be filed by one of the following systems:

- Client. Each client has a specially coded set of files for everything related to that client.

- Category. Set up files by industry or activity.

- Chronology. Set up monthly files.

⊞ Keep your "To Be Filed" tray on top of the file cabinets or on a shelf, preferably behind you. Just get it off the desk, where you may be endlessly tempted to rummage through it.

⊞ Crossing things off "To Do" lists has been scientifically proven to produce endorphins, so do not restrict yourself to wimpy cross-outs: Once you've completed a task, boost your mood by drawing a big fat line through the sucker. And if you forget to write something down that you've already finished, why deprive yourself of joy? Go ahead and post it after the fact, *then* cross it off.

⊞ Make a solemn vow to treat yourself after completing a big, complicated, exhausting, or unpleasant task. Don't worry about whether it's a "bribe" or a "reward." If going to an afternoon movie, playing golf, getting a facial, or soaking up some sun (wearing sunblock, of course) gets you off the dime, go ahead and make that promise to yourself — then make sure you keep it, so you don't end up harboring an intrapsychic grudge.

⊞ Before adopting someone else's work flow, let yourself experiment with different systems for getting and staying organized. The very best organizing system is the one that fits your learning style and pace.

Learning theorists have identified more than one way to recognize, absorb, and process information. As it turns out, you can accomplish almost anything more easily and with less stress if you know your particular learning style.

- If you tend to get a *feel* for situations; are *moved* by a thought or idea; and prefer hands-on demonstrations for equipment or techniques, then you're primarily *kinesthetic.*
- If you tend to *hear* what others are saying; enjoy audio tapes; or prefer verbal instructions, you're primarily *auditory.*
- If you tend to *see* other points of view or what others mean; can *see* the end result; or prefer graphs, charts, and pictures, you're primarily *visual.*

Rarely is someone exclusively one of these. We generally learn and remember by using a blend, although one will be dominant.

If you're primarily kinesthetic: Budget daily time to write out a "To Do" list, using writing instruments and materials that have tactile appeal. Desktop files or shallow desk trays will probably work well for you. Print out e-mail and file the hard copy.

If you're primarily kinesthetic, but also visual: Consider writing out a weekly master list of everything you need to do. Include a special section in which you list your top three goals. At the end of each week, highlight what still needs to be done, or simply copy it onto the next week's master list. Keeping desktop files or desk trays within sight will be important for you.

If you're primarily visual: Post sticky notes with information, instructions, or tasks in your sight line and flight path. Use colors and stickers to code what needs to be done and when. Month-at-a-glance calendars or charts will work well for you, as will electronic systems with lots of icons. Electronic filing systems for documents and correspondence should help.

If you're primarily visual, but also auditory: Use an electronic system that allows you to add sound effects to whatever is on the screen.

If you're primarily auditory: Talk to yourself out loud and immediately start cultivating visual and kinesthetic sensitivities!

⊠ Entire industries rely on fake deadlines to get anything done. Perhaps you already build extra time into deadlines you give others. (If you don't, try it, and feel your teeth unclench.)

⊠ If you're having trouble keeping your own deadlines, try faking yourself out. How? Post an early deadline on your calendar in a bright, attention-getting color and the "real" one in a more subdued tone.

⊠ Instead of driving yourself nuts by trying to Do It All, develop priorities by checking what needs to be done against short-term and long-term goals. Before plunging into anything, ask whether the activity will support these goals, or leach time and energy from them.

⊠ Choose some way of indicating directly on your "To Do" list which tasks are:

• Vitally important.

• Important but not critical.

• Quick no-brainers.

• Off-loadable.

⊠ It really doesn't matter whether you use letters, numbers, colors, or symbols. Just choose something and use it so consistently that you're able to tell at a glance what needs to be done first.

⊠ Have fun creating coding systems. Any bozo can use red to mean "high priority," green for "billing." Clown around at a local stationery store or wherever kids get stickers. Stock up on stars, hearts, arrows, insects, and animals. Then enjoy creating codes that not only work, but also lift your spirit.

⊠ Some top executives claim the car is a great place to hatch ideas, but don't use it this way unless you're stopped in traffic. Truly, the world does not need yet another spaced-out driver behind the wheel.

⊠ If you're feeling bored and able to arrange this, try:

• Working on-site at a client or customer's office.

• Setting up shop at the public library for a day or two.

• Heading for the backyard with your laptop computer and portable phone.

Sometimes a brief change of venue is just what you need to get juiced about what you do.

⊠ Schedule a monthly "Ruthless Day" during which you commit up to three hours to an uninterrupted blitzkrieg through your office. Use this time to clean out files, update address lists, clip articles from magazines (if you don't already do that when they arrive), transfer or delete stuff from the hard drive, and super-duper clean equipment.

⊞ Establish clear rules for how and when, if ever, you may be interrupted by family members in your office. Some suggestions for training them:

- Tell them a closed door always means "do not disturb," or "knock first." Post a note on your (closed) office door as a reminder.

- Post a sign with clock hands to indicate when you'll become available.

- Install an intercom. (There are good-quality wireless ones around.)

- Ask family members to call you from another line, like they'd have to if you were working elsewhere. (You do have at least two lines, don't you?)

⊞ Learn, then use, the language of boundaries with people outside as well as within your family:

- "Let me get back to you on that."

- "Let's schedule time now for a future conversation."

- "I'm on a deadline." (If you're a writer, it's cooler to say, "I'm on deadline.")

- "No."

That last word seems to be particularly difficult for speakers and listeners alike. If you tend to avoid saying "no," you may need to examine why under the lens of psychology.

⊞ If you think you're being clear but feel ignored, another bit of self-inquiry may be required. Is voice tone or body language undermining your message? Does your listener simply not understand that working from home is real work? If so, saying "I don't have the time," will eventually get the point across — if you say it often enough.

⊠ Help yourself get started more quickly and efficiently by noting where you left off and what you need to do next. Write a quick memo to yourself or highlight your computer text, giving yourself directions in brackets. Creative types recommend leaving something enough undone so that finishing it will prime the pump for more during the next work stint.

⊠ Having trouble getting started or sticking to whatever you're supposed to be doing? Make a list of how and when you get sidetracked. Awareness is the first step you must take before you can hope to change behavior, and this exercise practically guarantees more consciousness the next time you're smacked in the face with temptation. Let yourself enjoy it. Don't just write out your list, sit down at the computer to compose one using different, goofy fonts. Create a collage of your top 10 distractions and post it near your desk.

⊠ Tight deadlines are great for completing short-term tasks. If you know you tend to lose consciousness while filing, roaming the Internet, or cleaning documents off the hard drive, give yourself 15 timed minutes to do as much as you can. Then stop.

⊠ Assign realistic time limits to tasks you need to accomplish during the day. So what's realistic? Some activities consume more time than you'd expect. Others take less time than you wish they would.

⊠ Write a time allotment next to each task on your "To Do" list. In the beginning, you may have to set an egg timer or alarm clock to get a more accurate sense of how long 5, 15, or 30 minutes actually takes.

> " I don't recommend talking to someone while looking at a computer screen. If you're bored or busy, I think it's better to find a way to get off the phone. Who are these experts that recommend doing several things at once? "
>
> *Joann,* copyeditor

⊠ When the mail arrives:

- Open everything that has to do with business immediately. Save all personal items such as invitations, letters, and consumer credit card bills for one of your breaks.

- If deluged, date-stamp everything. This is especially important if your business involves filling orders.

- Sort by priorities and keep your hands off anything that isn't urgent and important.

⊠ Address envelopes without wasting time with your printer by using window envelopes or preprinted labels.

⊠ Get a telephone headset with an extra-long cord so your hands are free to do something else (quiet) while on the phone, such as:

- Signing papers and checks.

- Misting plants.

- Clipping articles.

- Updating lists.

- Folding laundry.

- Balancing the checkbook.

- Dusting the office.

- Filing papers or your fingernails.

But be careful: What psychologists call "polyphasing" can be dangerous. The more brain power you drain, the more you stress your nervous system. While it's certainly more efficient to do more than one thing at a time, you lose the advantages of doing this if you attempt too many higher-order tasks at once.

⊠ Borrow an organizing tip from the advertising industry and create "job jackets" for big projects. Use anything that will neatly contain all project-related research, memos, invoices, and miscellaneous notes in one place. Accordion-pleated file folders, large clasp envelopes, or dual-pocket folders work well. This is also a great way to recycle those sturdy cardboard envelopes used by delivery services. Jot key names, addresses, and phone numbers directly on the job jacket.

⊠ You'd be surprised at how much you can delegate — and to whom — even if you have a home office and work alone. But be careful to distinguish family chores from work-related tasks your kids might be persuaded to do for cash or barter:

- Persuade preteens to help with mailings.
- Let driving-age kids take the car in exchange for runs to the store, post office, etc.
- Make everyone responsible for cleaning his or her own room and tidying up after meals and snacks. Hey, if they can master Nintendo, they can learn how to start a dishwasher, washing machine, or clothes dryer.

⊠ Kids (and sometimes adult partners) need an obvious, visible, and audible way to gauge time. If you have to make or take business calls during "their" time, set a timer so they have a way of knowing when you'll be available to them. For this to work, they have to agree to leave you totally alone while you're talking, and you have to promise to get off the phone promptly when the buzzer goes off.

⊠ If you can afford to, set up two computers in your home office so your kids can quietly do homework, pursue on-line research, or even play computer games (with the sound off) if you work during what they consider "their" time.

Just because creativity seems magical, elusive, and totally independent from cognitive thought doesn't mean it can't be stimulated, cultivated, and nurtured. Like anything else, creativity flourishes when practiced regularly under the right conditions.

Creative woolgathering is different from sitting down with a specific situation in mind. Where, when, and how do you do your best deep thinking?

- Do you need silence, darkness, or solitude?
- Does the contemplative pace of needlecrafts, fishing, cooking, or woodworking allow your imagination to soar?
- Does the relative solitude of solo travel give your mind space to expand?
- Have you always done your best thinking in the bathtub? Walking in the woods? Staring at the ocean? Gazing at mountains?

What stimulates your creativity?
If you're primarily visual, try:
- Collecting clippings, notes, pictures, sketches, and cartoons.
- Scribbling on a dry-erase board with colored markers.
- Word games, crossword puzzles, and math puzzlers.

If you're primarily kinesthetic, while you're thinking, try:
- Juggling balls or beanbags.
- Rocking in a hammock or rocking chair.
- Putting together a jigsaw puzzle upside down as well as right-side up.
- Stroking the pet while staring into middle distance.

If you're primarily auditory, try:
- Free associating into a microcassette recorder.
- Listening to lots of different kinds of music.
- Asking yourself — and answering — questions such as:

What if I change this to become . . .

Bigger   Smaller   Lower   Shorter
Lighter   Wider   Thicker

What if everything were . . .

Reversed   Flipped
Turned inside out   Expanded

What else . . .

Could be done with this
Is like this
Could be added
Could be removed or eliminated

What if I tried a new or different . . .

Look   Shape   Color   Form
Ingredient   Part   Mechanism

Once you've discovered the optimal time and conditions for creative woolgathering:

- Book a regular appointment with yourself to wander around in your mind uninterrupted.
- Establish a quota for ideas.
- Set — and keep — deadlines for coming up with ideas.

In the meantime:

- Keep a pad and something to write with next to your bed, in the car, in the bathroom, or kitchen. Use pencil; it won't blob ink. If you're auditory, keep a microcassette recorder handy. There's even a gadget that combines a pen with a voice recorder.
- Write down the essence or spark of your idea, a key word or words that'll bring it all back when you have more time to flesh it out.
- Date all ideas, noting the time, if possible, to help you recognize when creative juices flow best.
- Use the day's endpoints for creative woolgathering. Instead of jumping immediately out of bed and flipping on the morning news, let your mind wander. Right before you go to bed, think or write about whatever it is you want to solve in your dreams.

⊠ While you're at it, duplicate your key office supplies (scissors, staplers, phone) in pint-size form.

⊠ Don't ditch child care just because you work at home. You'll need it more than ever. Fortunately, you probably have more options than you'd suspect:

- Live-in help, which could include grandparents or other relatives.

- Part-time sitters, which could include an older sibling.

- Part-time "mother's helpers," who would also be responsible for doing light housework and meal preparation.

- School-based after-school activities.

- Organized youth groups.

- Neighborhood-based cooperative or trading arrangements.

⊠ Instead of spending money on a baby-sitter, spend time with your kids and put the bucks toward part-time office help for tasks that don't require a lot of supervision.

⊠ After you finish composing a work schedule for yourself, make a copy for your family. To firmly plant the highlights of your work week in their heads (as well as yours), read the schedule out loud to them before sticking it to the refrigerator with magnets you so generously let them select.

⊠ Set aside things you can do after the kids go to bed. Depending on your own biorhythm, this may be the stuff that requires deep concentration, or things that you can do in a semifog.

One caution: Watch your time carefully so you don't end up putting in a full double day.

⊠ If you have full-time child care, create clear rules about when, why, and how often you'll see your kids during the workday. Remember, if you were working in someone else's office, you'd only see them in emergency situations or for an occasional special school event. In the long run, it'll be less confusing and upsetting for everyone — you, your caregiver, and your children — if you set up rules for contact, then stick to them.

> **"** My daughter is my assistant, but the mother-daughter thing doesn't get in the way. I can sense when she needs to talk with me as a daughter. Often when she seems frustrated I realize that she needs me to be a Mom, so we get out of the office for a walk or for dinner. What's interesting is that now we'll get so caught up in work that we need to take time out to do that. **"**
>
> *Victoria,* **independent producer**

⊠ It doesn't necessarily have to be on the weekend, but you do have to schedule at least one full day off for yourself — even if you have a major project due.

⊠ Do not let little voices in your head insist you don't have time to take time off. It's a documented fact that high productivity is tied to pacing, efficiency, and zest, all of which disappear in the presence of exhaustion.

⊠ Avoid the temptation of letting work cut into your personal downtime by establishing a quitting-time ritual:

• Establish a definite time to stop the day's work activities.

• Take time to clear your desk and reorganize your "To Do" list for the next day. If you have a work-in-progress, note where to pick it back up when you return.

• Mentally — or, if it's been a really rough one, actually — write a review of your accomplishments for the day.

- Thank the universe, God, or whatever you call the force greater, wiser, and more compassionate than you for the privilege of having work to do and a home office to do it in.

- Bid your plants and gadgets good night, turn off the lights, then leave. Be sure to shut the door (if you have one) behind you.

- Go splash water on your face, rinse your hands, or, if you have the time and inclination, pop into a warm bath before moving on to the next set of activities.

WHEN TO HIRE AN EXPERT

You've tried every system ever devised to organize your desk, your files, your billings, your work schedule, and still you feel like an inefficient slob. Contact the National Association of Professional Organizers (NAPO) for a referral.

4 Making the Transition from Their Office to Yours

What looks like a hot new trend — working from home — is really quite a traditional way to earn a living. Remember what you learned in eighth-grade social studies in between doodling cartoons on your notebook cover? Here's a quick review that'll place you way ahead of almost any high school graduate.

Until the Industrial Revolution, just about everyone worked from home, or at least lived in squalor above the shop. By the end of the 19th century, work (both how and where it was done) had become significantly transformed because of inventions (e.g., the steam engine), discoveries (e.g., interchangeable parts), changes in political economy (e.g., the rise of capitalism), and shifts in ideology (e.g., linking salvation to hard work rather than grace). Manufacturing and assembly now took place in factories. Almost everything else connected to working shifted to offices, and with that emerged the task of managing whomever performed these functions. Bureaucracy developed as an organizational form. Labor laws were written and passed. Family-based tasks like education were turned over to public institutions. Labor unions formed to protect workers from exploitation. Everyone worked outside the home — or so it seemed, even though at least some people have worked from home throughout the centuries, including the 20th.

So here we are at the turn of another century and work (both how and where it is done) is going through another upheaval of sorts. Now, the revolutionary technological changes of the late-20th century make it possible to perform *office-based* work from virtually anywhere. And that "anywhere" turns out to be "from home" for a growing number of people in a wide range of occupations — including you!

These days there are myriad options, which range from working full-time at your own home-based business to working part-time from your home office for an outside employer. The tips in this chapter make no assumptions about where you are currently located on this continuum. Sooner or later you'll have to make many of the same decisions — whether you're starting your own business or setting up a home office as a liberated employee.

This chapter zooms in on the issue of all issues when it comes to working from home: Is this work style the right one for you? Before you eagerly rewire your rumpus room, use this chapter to sort through the liabilities and benefits — both real and imagined — of setting up a home office.

The short answer is: Anyone who wants to and can swing it.

Among those who want to are not only those free spirits who have, for one reason or another, opted out of the rodent race. There are also people starting second careers, retirees, and entrepreneurial types who never had any illusions about fitting into the structured world of work. Add to that folks who want to spend more time with their families, plus anyone who wants to "moonlight," and you're looking at a hefty percentage of the working population.

Technology has so expanded our ability to work anywhere that it's actually easier to craft a list of what *cannot* be done from a home than it is to generate a truly comprehensive list of home-based businesses.

Generally speaking, you cannot run a business from home that involves vast teams of workers, lethal weapons, acres of space, dangerous chemicals, controlled substances, massive quantities of food, or heavy machinery. So you can forget about pouring concrete, performing periodontal surgery, mixing explosives, testing new drugs on a herd of lab rats, conducting weapons training, officiating basketball, and slaughtering livestock. Otherwise, you can start almost anything in today's phone/fax/modem world of business — from your kitchen table, if need be.

⊠ Take a personal finance course at your local community college or adult education program. Chances are you won't be able to get your business finances in order if your personal finances are a mess. You can easily accomplish this while still on someone else's payroll.

⊠ If you're starting your own business, be prepared to work long and hard for quite a while.

⊠ Timing is everything. If you're starting your own business in addition to setting up a home office, give yourself:

- Six months (and probably more) to get started. You may be able to pick up work fairly quickly after deciding to go this route, but that doesn't mean you'll have a highly functioning office overnight. It takes planning and preparation to pull together a home office that works well.

- A full year, at least, to settle into the flow of your business. Even if you've done scads of research, you'll need to experience an entire 12-month cycle of marketing, selling, producing, and billing to get a more accurate sense of what's possible.

- A financial cushion that will take care of living expenses for at least six months, but preferably a year if you can swing it.

⊠ Know thyself! Check your motives for wanting to work from a home office. Don't get all hung up in evaluating these motives, just know what they are. Knowing why you want to work from home will help you understand if that's what you really should be doing. It's surprisingly easy to mismatch problems and solutions.

If, for example, you want to work out of a home office because you think your boss is an incompetent yutz, then maybe you need to find another job (or get an attitude adjustment). If, however, you find that your best work emerges from solitude and silence, then working where you control the environment makes sense.

⊠ Ease yourself into working from home and developing business by:

- Building your own business while remaining someone else's employee. If you choose this approach you'll need to be discreet; maintain the level of quality and productivity your employer has come to expect; and conduct yourself with integrity, especially if you're planning to go solo in the same business or industry.

- Working at a part-time job to provide income and benefits while building your own business the rest of the time. In some instances, you may be able to turn your existing full-time job into a part-time one.

- Transforming your employer into your first client by showing how there's money to be saved by making you a contract consultant rather than a payroll employee.

- Graciously letting your spouse or significant other be the sole income provider until your business shows some financial stability. This might require you to simplify your current lifestyle to reduce financial burdens. If it's any consolation, all the great spiritual traditions see simplicity and temperance as virtues.

Telecommuting sounds good to you. You like your company, your job, your salary, and your benefits. You'd like everything much more if you could work from home some of the time. You know you could manage your job perfectly well and probably be more productive from home, but your employer insists that you have a presence in the office.

Before you can negotiate effectively, you'll need to identify your boss's worst fears. Do not get into evaluating these fears or rushing to dismiss them as unfounded. You can express empathy without being in agreement. Your negotiating position will, in fact, improve dramatically the moment you acknowledge such fears as being of legitimate concern to your employer. Empathy for her situation will turn your negotiation into a conversation rather than an adversarial procedure. This is a good thing.

Your first goal, then, is to engage your boss in a conversation — or series of conversations — at the end of which you are able to agree that telecommuting is mutually beneficial.

So what's the big-deal problem with your working from home? If you ask this question directly, come from a place of curiosity. Keep your voice neutral and conversational as you say something like, "Help me understand your concerns about telecommuting." And for heaven's sake, do not loom over your boss with arms akimbo.

You may, however, want to enter into this discussion with a little more appreciation for your boss's position. Productivity is the number one concern for most managers and underlies other expressed worries, such as:

- You'll become unmanageable.
- Quick, efficient communication will become impossible.
- You'll miss essential water cooler conversation and ad hoc lavatory conferences.
- Everyone else in the office will want to do it.
- It will look unprofessional to clients and customers.

- *Her* bosses will think she's a pushover, unable to control her people.
- The company won't get the dollar value of a full day's work out of you.
- Accountability will go down the tubes, which in turn will screw up the monthly numbers.

You'll probably need to respond to some, if not all, of these points, but do not attempt to rebut each one in real time. Instead, admit you've been given a lot to think about and that you'd like to respond at some point in the near future. Then go off and gather whatever information you need to turn these into nonissues. Before getting the go-ahead to telecommute, you'll need to:

- Separate what can be done at home from what must be done in the office to determine how much time you'll need to spend in both places. Generate a written list of tasks.
- Come up with a mutually satisfactory definition of what constitutes a "presence" in the office. Plan to show up at least once every week and for important powwows. Generate a written list of key meetings.
- Develop a transition plan that eases you into telecommuting and calms everyone down. Generate a written schedule for two or three months during which you telecommute one or two days a week.
- Find out what you'll need in the way of equipment and furniture. If you already have the equipment, great. This will strengthen your position. Generate a written plan for forwarding calls, using voice mail, e-mail, facsimile communications, and the company intranet.

After you get the go-ahead, be:

- Darn sure to do everything you promised to do.
- Scrupulous at documenting your efforts and results.

> **"** The transition to my own business from my home office was pretty smooth because I took some projects with me. What was difficult was setting up all the business structures.
>
> "Sometimes I miss being in the office with the structure and even the commute, but I also think that may just be a case of the grass seeming greener elsewhere. **"**
>
> *Elizabeth,* literary agent

⊞ Start the sales pitch for working from home *after* you land an interview (or get a call-back). In some instances, you may be able to make a compelling proposal part of your cover letter. (Include your office capabilities in your résumé.)

⊞ If you're using an executive placement professional, make your interest in telecommuting known.

⊞ Stick to your regular hours and rhythms when you first start working from home, even if you know you'll be changing your schedule to comfort-fit at some point. This will help reinforce the fact that you're still working, not on vacation. Once that reality sinks in, come up with a schedule that makes sense for you. (See also chapter 3.)

⊞ Educate neighborly neighbors about your work schedule and time availability. This is especially important if, before you got busy with business, you had a long-standing tradition of sharing morning or afternoon coffee. Be sure to let them know under what circumstances they're welcome to ring your doorbell during the day.

If there are items they may always borrow without checking — the garden hose, your grill, your teenager — tell them what they are to reduce the frequency of possible interruptions.

Fear is an uncomfortable emotion. But some fears that may appear to have a toehold in reality may be a distortion of it. Cognitive therapists help clients chuck such distortions in favor of reality. They say that identifying distortions and developing "rational responses" to them will significantly calm you down.

Of the basic cognitive distortions that have been identified, there are several that, separately or together, will sabotage your transition to a home office. (See the "Quick Definitions" box on page 80.)

After contemplating the following fears, come up with your own, then generate rational responses. In other words, talk back to yourself (in writing) as if you were a rational, fearless human being.

Fear:

I won't make enough money.

Rational response:

You'll make as much money as you need to make.

First of all, expenses will go way down. Second, because you're working from home, you might not care as much about making big bucks. Admit it, didn't you often demand more money to offset your resentments about the corporate work scene?

Fear:

No one will take me seriously.

Rational response:

Take yourself seriously and others will, too. What you're doing is serious. It's your life and your livelihood, after all.

Fear:

I'll lose my secure income and job benefits.

Rational response:

There is no such thing as a secure income and benefits. Ever hear of downsizing? It's the latest bizspeak for "layoffs." Entire industries are being decimated, and even if they weren't, most people change jobs every 2½ years anyway. How is having to add a new client or two any less stable than waiting for the ax to fall?

You may think you're seeing clearly, but there's a much-better-than-average chance that if you're having uncomfortable feelings, your thinking is out of whack with what's really going on in the present, or will in the future. Through which of these cognitive distortions do you tend to filter reality?

1. All-or-Nothing Thinking: There is no such thing as balance. Everything is either wonderful or stinky. If you're not the best, you're the worst. They'll either love your work, or think you're a hack.

2. Overgeneralization: One blooper or bummer is incontrovertible evidence of future failure. If *they* don't give financing for the project, no one ever will. Akin to this is Labeling and Mislabeling, wherein you attach the most damning label in the most flamboyantly hysterical language to yourself or others. You catch your own bookkeeping error and mutter "what a total jerk" to yourself. A supplier delivers something late and you vow never to order another thing from those "con artists" again. (In reality you use more extreme language, which is unprintable in a book of this quality.)

3. Disqualifying the Positive: Good things don't mean squat. Compliments don't count and praise is probably gratuitous. Just because you've won industry awards for the past 10 years doesn't mean you'll ever land clients of your own.

4. Magnification (Catastrophizing)/Minimization: You either exaggerate or underestimate the importance of things. You got a letter from the local zoning board, so that means you'll never be able to do business from your home. Your major client is a major P.I.T.A., but it's really no big deal: You'll just munch antacids every time you work on that account.

5. Personalization: You actually think you cause things to happen for which you have no real responsibility. It's all your fault that your brother-in-law had to declare personal bankruptcy while you were busy trying to get your business off the ground.

*Adapted from "Definitions of Cognitive Distortions" (Table 3–1) in David D. Burns, *Feeling Good: The New Mood Therapy* (New York: William Morrow and Company, Inc., 1980).

⊠ Go to the library, cruise the Net, and hang out in a bookstore that lets you flip through the merchandise to read up on saving money. In the finance section you'll find a growing number of texts about how to achieve financial independence and stability without having to earn (or spend) scads of money.

⊠ Did you sign a contract with a "noncompete" clause while working for someone else? If so, this may prevent you from approaching your former (employer's) clients. On the other hand, whatever you signed might not have any real legal clout. Check with your attorney.

⊠ Making your case for working from home may be easier than you'd think if:

- Your company already allows its sales representatives to maintain home offices. In this instance, you'll need to make a case for why your job can be done just as effectively as theirs can from home.

- You're a senior-level manager who has a long, unsullied history of working diligently without supervision. Having a reputation for masterful delegation will also help.

- You have technical skills or add such special value to the organization that they'll do almost anything to accommodate your quirky habits or needs.

⊠ If you're looking for employment and want to work from home, don't give up on want ads for full-time, outside office-based employment. You may be able to persuade prospective employers that they'll be getting a great employee at a great deal if you prove at the outset that you have not only the skills to do the job, but also the means of doing the job well from a home office.

- You're highly self-motivated and persistent. Mommy never had to haul you out of bed for school and employers have always characterized you as a "self-starter." People are more likely to tell you to "give it a rest" than to "get into gear." You're willing to stay with a project long after everyone else is falling over with fatigue and frustration.
- You enjoy solitude. You have intense privacy needs, especially when working. You're never bored and see nothing wrong with relating almost exclusively via e-mail. You're not exactly misanthropic, it's just that you find people disruptive.
- Authority gives you the creeps unless, of course, you're in charge. You grew horns, then locked them with every boss you ever had. Subordinates considered you somewhat of a benign dictator. You're willing to concede this may be a core therapeutic issue but don't care to work on it.
- When you first heard that "God is in the details," you thought that meant it was okay to micromanage. Your boss thought you weren't using time wisely. Your assistant was only too happy to let you dive for your own phone. You're willing, in theory, to off-load some tasks, but chicken out at the last minute because you can do them better and faster. Administrative details aren't demeaning; they allow you to know what's going on.
- Uncertainty doesn't throw you into a panic. Truth to tell, you find it kind of exciting. You were legendary around the office for perking up while everyone else was flipping out. You have a very high tolerance for ambiguity.
- Flexibility is important to you. You've always been a spurt worker, gathering ideas and energy for later harvesting. You never understood, let alone adhered to, office rules about coffee breaks and lunch hours. If you ruled the world of work, you'd let everyone get work done by optimizing her individual biorhythm.

- You derive identity and satisfaction from a job title and a place on the organization chart. You truly believe that a tree falling in the forest with no one around does not make a sound.
- Security and stability are more important to you than food, sleep, or sex. You don't care if it's all an illusion. Your mother hid your blankie when you were four and your father came of age during the Great Depression. There's not enough therapy in the world to make you feel secure. You need a place to go every day and a regular paycheck.
- You are revitalized by gossip and office intrigue. You want to hear the latest jokes delivered live. Truth to tell, you go a little nuts if there isn't a lot of social stimulation. Perhaps that's why you end up organizing the company pig roast every year.
- Structure keeps you on task. You simply work better when you know the roles and rules. You prefer being guided and supervised by someone else. You're fine with accountability, just not for everything. Let someone else be in charge.
- Given the choice between working on a team and solo projects, you'll always choose the team. What you cook up in a group is always better than what you do on your own. Your bosses adored you because you took direction without getting huffy, deferred to others as appropriate without fanfare, and didn't go grubbing for high-profile assignments.
- Certain aspects of work are simply beneath you. You'll be darned if you'll give up your secretary, even though he's not too swift. You'd much prefer not knowing where equipment and supplies come from. You want a bevy of subordinates onto whom you can off-load whatever you want. The mere thought of having to do everything yourself makes your flesh crawl.

⊠ You may find yourself working overtime more often from your home office than you ever did at an outside office. If you're still on someone else's payroll, keep accurate records of your work hours to help you assess whether you've inadvertently reduced your pay to below minimum wage.

⊠ Being on your own does not mean doing everything yourself. It's perfectly okay to hire an expert, or simply an extra set of hands if you need help. In fact, you ought to make sure you've budgeted the money to bring someone in from the outside if:

• A technical problem emerges that you have neither time, energy, nor enough personal knowledge to solve.

• Massive amounts of paperwork threaten to bury you.

• Tight deadlines make it impossible for you to comfortably and sanely handle your normal workload.

• There's stuff you just can't stomach doing by or for yourself.

Snide comments about home-based workers not being in the "real world" are way off the mark. My real world includes shopping, cooking, laundry, doctor's appointments, oil changes, prayer time, veterinarian visits, and other family emergencies, plus clients and colleagues who experience these same things.

What's so "real" about rolling out of bed at a ridiculous hour to dress up in uncomfortable clothes, only to stress out in traffic on the way to an office that, if it has any to begin with, has windows that won't open? What's so "real" about trying to be productive during an arbitrary set of work hours that were established as optimal during the early 1900s? What's so "real" about jamming everything else into evenings and weekends? I'd really like to know.

5 Managing Body, Soul, and Spirit

It's strange, but true! Lots of good work can be accomplished without tension headaches, a stiff neck, frozen shoulder muscles, seething resentments, and zero tolerance for anything by midafternoon. You need not wreck your entire being to balance your checkbook, deliver a service, or meet deadlines — unless, of course, you're dysfunctional enough to want to.

Believe me, I spent years working at a pace and level of intensity that decimated my health without increasing my output or enhancing any of my relationships. How could I nurture my whole self if I didn't even know I had one? Like most other people, I hadn't developed a refined understanding of what constituted my "whole being."

Eventually I learned that in addition to having a physical body and an active mind, I had access to a source of wisdom that far exceeded my mere human existence. My felt awareness of this reality didn't click into place all at once. It took some time before I understood how my mind used my body to transmit messages. Soon thereafter I realized the impact that my physical condition had on my mood and behavior. Much later it finally dawned on me that I wasn't In Charge of Everything in the Universe, but that's another story.

This attention to the entire being — body, mind, soul, and spirit — is what is meant by holistic living. Incidentally, this balanced and integrated approach to life is as old as the hills (or at least Greek civilization), despite its trendy woo-woo crunchy granola image.

Taking a more holistic approach to work makes good sense for those of us who always or occasionally work from home. Surely you did not opt for a home office to get bleary-eyed from staring at the computer monitor, to blob out from junk food, or to hurl curses at your basset hound. Nor did you return home to pulverize whatever remained of your soul and spirit.

Maybe creating a more holistic lifestyle wasn't your number one reason for setting up a home office, but surely it was somewhere on your wish list, even if you didn't exactly call what you wanted "holistic."

Page through this chapter to find tips for keeping your entire being healthy, happy, and whole while you work in your home office. In addition to tips about food, fitness, and relaxation, there's information in here that'll explain why you either keel over or come to life during certain hours of the day. This chapter also gives you permission to nap.

⊞ Water is probably the most essential element in our bodies. Consider this: Our thoughts swim around in an organ that's 75 percent liquid, so at the very least, you really don't want your brain to dehydrate.

To stay healthily hydrated, drink at least eight 8-ounce glasses of liquid a day. Start first thing in the morning with two tall glasses of water or a big mug of hot water and lemon.

Sorry, but coffee, tea, cocoa, and soft drinks with cola don't count, because caffeine is dehydrating.

⊞ Instead of hoisting a half-gallon bottle of water every time you need a refill, get your very own water cooler. Call bottled-water companies for information about this equipment, which can be as simple as a bottle on a crock tap, or as elaborate as a hot and cold dispenser. You can also buy pitcher filter systems that will fit neatly on a bookshelf or file cabinet.

⊞ Consider using a humidifier if the air in your office is excessively dry (an increase of static electricity is one indicator) and you always feel cold.

Look for a unit that's compact and quiet so you don't add noise pollution to your environmental woes. Some units will also clean the air; others are designed to minimize the growth of mold and algae within the water tank. Ultrasonic units are probably your best bet, but be sure to look for one with a demineralizing filter. Regular tap water and even distilled water will throw teensy particles of minerals into the air you breathe.

Since all humidifiers are a mixed blessing for people with sensitivities to allergens, shop wisely.

⊞ Add an electronic air purifier to your heating and cooling system, or get a portable one for your office. These cleaners remove airborne dust and smoke. However, they don't remove airborne gas molecules, so if you work with a lot of chemicals, you'll have to explore air exhaust systems as well.

▣ Look for air purifiers that circulate air through either a HEPA filter ("high-efficiency particulate arresting") or an electrostatic filter that treats more air per minute.

▣ Reawaken anytime throughout the day by engaging in diligent dental hygiene:

- Brush your teeth with a super-minty toothpaste. Peppermint enhances alertness.

- Floss each and every tooth. Remember to drag some floss behind your rear molars.

- Clean your tongue by gently dragging the side of a soup spoon over your taste buds, if you don't own a special tongue scraper.

- Swish mouthwash through your teeth.

▣ Perk up with a midday shower. If you shower in a tub, it's easy to create a fragrant steam bath. Let hot water run for a minute with the door shut to steam up the bathroom. Right before stepping into the shower, plug the drain so a few inches of water collect, then add no more than four drops of an invigorating essential oil. See the aromatherapy box on pages 90–91 for specific tips about which oils to use for what.

▣ Need to simmer down? Don't wait until the end of the day. Soak in a tub filled with warm (not hot) water for 20 minutes. For a super zone-out, bathe by candlelight with prepared bath salts or add no more than eight drops of your own relaxation mixture.

▣ Dunk a clean washcloth into a sink basin of water into which you've stirred essential oils, then press it against your face and neck. (In general, cool water is revitalizing and warm water is relaxing, although maybe not for you. Experiment.) Breathe in and let the aroma help you energize or unwind, depending on the scents. Repeat this facial compress a dozen times.

"Aromatherapy."

The very word brings to mind images of sweet-smelling sachets tucked into the linen closet, a glowing host of fragrant candles on the night table, or the perfumed ministrations of a gentle spa facialist. There's nothing wrong with this list, except you forgot to include the scents that make working pleasurable as well as productive. If your office smells like office supplies, leftover coffee, your mid-afternoon snack, and brain waves, it's time to expand your olfactory horizons.

You can buy commercial air fresheners, but why not control the quality, intensity, and effectiveness by creating your own with pure essential oils? These highly concentrated extracts are available in small quantities that make it easy for you to experiment with different synergistic blends. Look for pure essential oils in dark glass, dropper bottles. They will vary in price according to scent. Splurge on higher-quality oils for your bath. You can get away with using something less expensive for air freshening.

Note: Use only one or two drops to start, and dilute with water. Pure essential oils are for external use only, so don't try tasting them, and keep them from direct contact with your skin.

Wake up and smell the . . .
> Eucalyptus
> Grapefruit
> Lemon
> Peppermint
> Rosemary

Not only are these scents invigorating, uplifting, and rejuvenating, but their essential oils are also known to have antiseptic and disinfectant properties. Peppermint and rosemary, in particular, are mental stimulants.

Slow down and sniff the . . .
> Chamomile
> Geranium
> Orange
> Palma rosa
> Sandlewood
> Ylang ylang

Stir six to eight drops to the bathwater just before you dip into the tub.

Blend for balance with . . .
> Bergamot
> Clary sage
> Lavender

Blend any of these essential oils with either the invigorating ones or relaxing scents. They will work synergistically to create balance.

How to use:
Save scented candles for the bedroom and bath unless you plan to vigilantly monitor the flame. Your office has too many flammable supplies, so you're much safer releasing scent into the air with:

- Diffusers: Available in pottery, porcelain, metal, and glass, these simmer pots slowly and gently heat the oil in a small basin of water, allowing the scent to diffuse into the air. You can find models that are electrically powered or heated by enclosed flame. Do not use more than 10 drops of pure essential oil at a time.
- Lightbulbs: Drip one to six drops of essential oil directly onto a lightbulb *before* you turn on the lighting fixture. Essential oils are too volatile to risk dripping them directly onto a hot bulb.
- Room spray: Fill an eight-ounce plant sprayer with warm water, add 10 to 15 drops of essential oil, then shake. Lightly mist curtains, fabric upholstery, and carpeting.

⊠ Breathe deeply to oxygenate your blood supply and revitalize your entire system. This is especially important if you find yourself sighing a lot. Take a brisk walk or do some other form of aerobic exercise if you like, but you can also:

- Sing heartily in the shower, at your desk, or while driving.

- Scream loudly into a towel or pillow (if anyone else is around), or in your the car with the windows closed. This is extremely satisfying if you're driving through a tunnel or at a railroad stop when a train passes by.

- Laugh uproariously at whatever you find hilarious. Keep silly stuff filed, pick up something funny to read, or rent a slapstick classic on video.

- Learn, then practice, one of the ancient yogic breathing exercises. Make sure that you choose the correct practice for the desired result. Some of these exercises will be stimulating; others will turn you into a puddinglike blob.

⊠ Go ahead and yawn your head inside out if you feel like it; who's watching? Yawning is one way the body releases stress and restores oxygen to the system. Stifling yawns simply isn't healthy. If you're unsure as to how to yawn well, spend some time watching cats or dogs wake up from one of their zillion, abundantly satisfying naps.

⊠ You'll also want to add air-purification devices and smokeless ashtrays to your list of essential office equipment. Avoid dropping ashes onto and into your other pieces of equipment.

In fact, you might move your printer to a nonsmoking area so that everything you produce is relatively odor-free. Did you know that smoke particles can damage disks and computers?

⊞ Improve the air quality in your office by hanging or placing one green plant per one hundred square feet. Ferns, philodendrons, dracaenae, pothos, and spider plants are especially good for reducing the amount of formaldehyde, benzene, and other airborne toxins.

Fortunately, these plants require minimal maintenance. They will thrive with scant light, weekly watering (and won't croak if you forget), and regular misting. In fact, overwatering these plants simply leads to mold and mildew being released into the air.

One note of caution: Philodendrons are highly toxic when eaten, so do not keep them within reach of small children or pets.

Here's a simple equation: Breath = Life.

According to the ancient yogis, not only does the breath bring more oxygenated blood to the brain, but it also plays a key role in controlling vital life energy, or *prana*. Many of the exercises that yogis use to prepare for meditation can help you enhance concentration, steady your emotions, relax, or boost vitality during the workday. All yogic breathing exercises require focusing on three elements of breating: inhaling, retaining the breath, and exhaling. (Ironically, inhaling is the least significant aspect of the practice.)

Here are a few basic breathing exercises for you to try:

Feeling sluggish?
- Sit comfortably with your spine straight. You may sit in a chair with your feet flat on the floor, or sit on the floor with your legs crossed.
- Take a few normal breaths, then inhale deeply through your nose, relaxing your abdominal muscles so your lungs fill fully with air.
- Now exhale forcefully and quickly through your nose by sharply contracting your abdominal muscles.
- Repeat this process 20 times, then inhale and exhale completely.
- Deeply and fully inhale again and hold until just before it becomes uncomfortable to do so, then exhale slowly and completely.

Feeling distracted?
- Sit, stand, or lie down comfortably.
- Breathe in deeply and fully through your nose for 5 counts.
- Hold your breath for 7 counts.
- Exhale slowly and completely through your slightly opened mouth for 11 counts.
- Repeat 12 times.

Feeling agitated?
- Lie down on the floor with a pillow underneath your knees, if need be, to keep your upper spine flat on the floor.
- Take in a deep full breath through your nose, letting your belly expand first, then your abdomen, and finally your chest.
- At the top of your breath, hold your breath for 7 counts.
- Exhale slowly, deliberately, and fully through your nose. During this exhale, you'll empty the breath out in reverse — lungs, then abdomen, then belly.
- Take a deep slow breath in and out, then repeat this three-part breath at least 6 times.

You can find other breathing practices described in any good yoga book, but do not experiment with any of the advanced techniques on your own. Find a qualified yoga teacher to give you a breathing lesson. Without proper instruction, these powerful exercises could make you a little goofy, or in some instances, absolutely nuts.

⊞ Are you still a smoker? Stop it! Not only does smoking cause cancer and respiratory diseases, but it absolutely robs your body of oxygen as well.

Addiction specialists say it's easier to kick crack cocaine than it is to clean out a nicotine habit, so quitting is tough work. Fortunately, there are any number of over-the-counter gradual withdrawal systems available these days, plus support groups that meet weekly for an hour of friendly whimpering about withdrawal, among other things.

⊞ If you absolutely refuse to quit smoking, forbid yourself to smoke while talking on the phone. Clients and customers can tell you're smoking by the shifts and catches in your breathing patterns. Not only does this confirm that you're not giving them your full attention, but it also tells them that you're under the thrall of an addiction.

⊞ Sleep! The Final Frontier. If you regularly sleep through your alarm and stumble around in a daze for 15 minutes to an hour after rolling out of bed, you're sleep-starved. You may need to do one or more of the following things:

• Sleep longer hours.

• Adjust your work schedule so you can sleep later.

• Go to sleep earlier.

• Stick to a more regular sleep schedule. Alas, sleeping later on weekends or one or two nights a week will not help you catch up. It will only confuse your body more. Regular sleeping hours work better.

Incidentally, it doesn't really matter which hours you sleep, you just need to have enough of them. Circadian rhythms — patterns of sleep and wakefulness — vary from individual to individual.

⊡ Taking a nap for 15 to 20 minutes will boost your energy and mood, help repair your nervous system, and enhance your creativity and productivity for hours. The best time to schedule a nap is after you've been awake for 8 hours, and 8 hours before tucking yourself in for the night.

⊡ You can boost the salutary benefits of a short snooze even more by:

• Taking it lying down.

• Breathing in deeply and slowly a few times right after you shut your eyes.

• Listening to soft music through a headset. In fact, there are subliminal relaxation tapes available made specifically for short naps.

• Draping a little herbal or husk pillow across your eyes.

⊡ Scheduling stress busters throughout the day is a healthier preventative approach than waiting until you're ready to commit suicide or homicide before scheduling a much needed break.

Set a kitchen timer, alarm clock, or watch beeper to remind you when to take short stress breaks during which you:

• Wander outside for a brisk, or slow, walk around the block.

• Meditate for 10 minutes by focusing your complete attention on something. Closing your eyes and noticing the rhythm of your breath is one easy way to meditate.

• Call a friend, preferably from your kitchen or living room phone, to chitchat about something non–work related for 10 minutes.

• Do your breathing and stretching exercises.

• Take a short but restful nap.

• Prepare and eat a healthful snack away from your desk.

Surely you remember this old saw: "Early to bed, early to rise makes a man healthy, wealthy, and wise." Setting aside the question as to whether the term "man" was intended to include women as well, I think it's safe to say that this advice seems to transcend culture.

If Ayurveda, Traditional Chinese Medicine, and Western medicine agree on anything, it's that going with the body's cyclical flow makes more sense than swimming against these natural tides. Recognizing and honoring one's biorhythm practically guarantees more alertness and productivity.

Although each system is based on different properties, all designate relatively similar activities to relatively similar times during any given 24-hour period. What's different is the way each system proposes to balance body, mind, and spirit as well as the means used (e.g., herbs vs. drugs) to regulate and heal. As a result, it's a lot easier to worship at one shrine than to mix these modalities, especially if there's a practitioner involved.

Ayurveda

India's five-thousand-year-old system of medicine, ayurveda, emphasizes the interrelationship of body, mind, and spirit. Practitioners focus on three primary metabolic body types, or *doshas*. The opposing energies of *vata* and *kapha* are mediated by *pitta*. The body functions harmoniously when vata, pitta, and kapha are balanced. Illness is a result of imbalances among these three doshas. Doshas not only reveal innate tendencies, but are also believed to correspond to ways of thinking, feeling, and behaving.

Since vata controls thoughts and emotions, you'll want to reserve any heavy-duty mental activities for "vata time" — 2:00 to 6:00 in the afternoon.

Because of the way pitta regulates digestion and metabolism, plan to eat your largest meal between 10:00 in the morning and 2:00 in the afternoon. Make sure you get to sleep by 10:00 at night.

Kapha maintains bones, muscles, and stamina, so schedule exercise between 6:00 and 10:00 in the morning.

Traditional Chinese Medicine

Traditional Chinese medicine, which has been practiced for over three thousand years, views the human body as both a reflection and a microcosm of nature. Emphasizing the interdependence and relationship of opposites such as hot and cold, dampness and dryness, yin and yang, practitioners seek to balance the body's elements by maintaining the smooth flow of life-force energy, or *chi* (*qi*). Organ-based energy cycles through the body's energy meridians every 3 hours during any 24-hour period. Optimal health and performance occur when yin and yang are in balance.

The energy of yin organs (heart, spleen, lungs, kidney, liver) is most prevalent between 6:00 in the evening and 6:00 in the morning. This is the best time for sleep and other quiet activities. Replenish the body with breakfast between 7:00 and 9:00 in the morning. Restore the body by preparing for sleep between 9:00 and 9:30 in the evening.

The energy of yang organs (small intestine, stomach, large intestine, bladder, gallbladder) is most prevalent between 6:00 in the morning and 6:00 in the evening. This is the best time for work and exercise.

Western Medicine

According to Western medicine, health and performance are tied to a number of cycles, known as circadian rhythms. Patterns of sleep and activity are all affected by body temperature, and the interrelationship of heart rate, blood pressure, and hormonal levels.

Western practitioners believe the optimal time to wake up is between 6:00 and 7:00 in the morning. Any major mental activity should be scheduled between 8:00 and noon because that's when body temperature is elevated. Plan to down the day's largest meal and rest between noon and 3:00 in the afternoon. Body temperature then rises again, so there's another good hour available for mental activity between 3:00 and 4:00.

As for exercise, it'll be most effective at the end of the day, when motor skills are high and muscles are already warmed up. Get to sleep by midnight and let the body restore itself with sleep between 1:00 and 5:00 in the morning.

- Stroke your pets, unless you have fish. Those you can watch (or meditate upon).

- Get down on your knees and have a silent chat with whatever power in the universe is greater, smarter, more compassionate, and more loving than you. Not a big believer in spiritual hooey? That's okay. Skip this suggestion, but consider coming back to it when you're so stressed out you think nothing on the earth plane will help.

- Log on to a special-interest bulletin board or a forum through one of the commercial on-line services.

⊠ After waking up, reorient yourself with a few more deep breaths and gentle stretches. If you kick into gear too abruptly, you'll undermine the wonderful benefits of napping.

⊠ If you're a morning bird, there are plenty of ways to start the day before actually sitting down at your desk:

- Schedule breakfast dates with friends and colleagues before they have to go to their offices.

- Take an early-morning exercise class or work out on your home equipment.

- During the summer, squeeze gardening or car washing in before it gets too hot.

⊠ Evil bean or faithful friend? Coffee, and the caffeine it contains, will:

- Dehydrate your body.

- Cause uncomfortable stomach-acid secretions after about four cups.

- Interfere with sleep cycles if imbibed after midday.

- Do nothing good for your menstrual cycle or your ability to tolerate those of the women in your life.

On the other hand: Two cups in the morning will increase alertness — temporarily.

⊞ Boohoo, coffee isn't the only thing loaded with caffeine. Watch out for chocolate, certain aspirin-like products, tea, soft drinks, and some prescription medications.

⊞ If you don't want to live or work without caffeine, try switching to green tea. It, at least, has cancer-preventative properties — but so does broccoli.

⊞ Keep whatever vitamins, minerals, herbs, or food supplements that can be taken between meals in a pill case in or near your desk, where you'll be more likely to remember to take them.

⊞ You may think you can get away with plowing through a few days and nights with minimal sleep, but you can't — not really. Return to your regularly scheduled sleep program as soon as possible.

If you've been working like a lunatic for weeks, clear the decks for a night or two of completely uninterrupted sleep. Otherwise, you'll most assuredly keel over. Maybe not immediately, but sooner than you think.

⊞ Keep a supply of homeopathic flower remedies handy for stressful situations and emergencies. The most popular and best-known of these is a Bach Flower Essence called "Rescue Remedy," which blends impatiens, star of bethlehem, cherry plum, rock rose, and clematis. Because these essences are in an alcohol tincture, they must be used with caution. Even someone without an alcohol problem will need to thoroughly dilute this remedy in a glass of water. It can also be applied topically to the skin.

Books and pamphlets about the correct use of flower essences are generally available at health food stores that stock wellness products.

Sometimes a short break just isn't enough to reboot your human hard drive. You may, in fact, need a more drastic change of pace or scenery — without making reservations, packing a bag, and leaving town.

If you desperately want to leave town, you're better off taking a long weekend. Those who study such things claim they're more psychologically and physically beneficial than a traditional two-week vacation.

Meanwhile, any one of these mini vacations will do wonders for your overall sense of well-being within a few hours:

- Visit a museum or a few art galleries. Make sure you include lunch or dinner out.
- Browse through a bookstore, preferably one with a wonderful tea shop.
- Spend an afternoon in the public library reading all the magazines you wish you had time to read.
- Race your car at the local track — *after* you take high-performance-driving lessons.
- See a local tourist attraction or national landmark you've never seen before.
- Take yourself to an afternoon movie, ballgame, or tennis match and feel free to blow a few bucks on snacks.
- Hike through nature or walk in a park. If this is too strenuous, rent a video nature tour instead.
- Schedule a half-day of beauty that includes a facial, manicure, and pedicure. If that doesn't appeal to you, detail your car.
- Register for a class or activity — hatha yoga, aerobics, arts and crafts, cooking, musical-instrument instruction, or voice lessons, for instance — that meets once or twice a week.
- Stay home, turn off the phones, and do absolutely nothing for at least four hours.

⊞ Designate a small shelf or surface for a periodically changing grouping of things that inspire you — pictures of loved ones (including yourself), a *chotchka* or two, dried flowers, a small replica of your favorite car of all time — whatever lifts your spirit.

If anyone accuses you of erecting a weird little altar, tell them it's a tableau. Or simply shrug.

⊞ Every month or so, reprogram the screen saver on your computer monitor with a new, helpful, and inspiring message or affirmation. Try:

• Remember to breathe . . .

• This too shall pass . . .

• Pace yourself . . .

• I have everything I need or want . . .

• Abundance surrounds me . . .

• Don't sweat the small stuff . . . It's all small stuff . . .

Don't worry about coming up with something original. Just come up with something that inspires you to stay balanced as you work.

⊞ Keep a supply of soft earplugs handy for when you need complete focus and concentration. If you travel a lot for business, don't forget to toss a few sets into your briefcase, purse, and carry-on luggage.

> **❝** Compared to the corporate world, my home office is an almost totally stress-free environment. Sure, there are deadlines, but that's nothing like the stress of constantly wondering about getting laid off, the politics, the back stabbing, and the total lack of efficiency. **❞**
>
> *Sarah,* **financial analyst**

⊞ If you position your computer monitor so that the top of the screen is at eye level or slightly below, you won't have to tilt your head and neck to see. Support your eyes and help preserve your vision with one or more of these suggestions:

- Place the monitor as far from your face as possible without losing readability. Twenty-four inches is supposed to be optimal.

- Enlarge on-screen icons enough to minimize squinting.

- If you already wear glasses, have a pair specially made for computer use.

- Make sure your monitor screen is wiped clean every day.

- Place your monitor at an angle to or away from bright light, and adjust the brightness accordingly.

- Use a glare screen to improve contrast.

- Buy a hood or fashion one out of cardboard, and tape it to the top of your monitor to reduce glare.

- Dim the ambient lighting.

- Remember to blink frequently, rest your eyes for 15 seconds every 15 to 20 minutes, and periodically lubricate your eyes with artificial tears.

⊞ Replicate natural light with full-spectrum lightbulbs. These bulbs, which come in both incandescent and fluorescent forms, are generally available in health food stores or by mail order from any number of healthy-living-product catalogs. They're expensive, but worth the extra cost if seeing true color is important to you and your work. Also, because they're like plant lights for people, those who use full-spectrum lights report having more energy and don't seem to get sick as often as those who use regular lighting.

Note: Full-spectrum lights do not provide the same benefits as artificial bright light. "Bright" lights that are 5 to 50 times brighter than ordinary ones are used specifically to treat the seasonal affective disorder (SAD) that hits many people during the darker days of winter.

⊞ Keep a small step stool under your desk to prop up your feet. You significantly reduce strain on your lower back when your knees are higher than your hips. Some specialty catalogs feature footrests that tilt and rock to help keep the blood circulating in your legs.

⊞ Avoid repetitive stress injuries at the computer keyboard by keeping your forearms horizontal and wrists straight. You may have to adjust the height of your desk, your chair, or your keyboard to achieve this.

⊞ Take a break from typing every hour at the very least. Use this time to exercise or massage your hands:

• Use your thumbs to massage each opposite hand in small, firm circles for 10 seconds. Begin at the base of your palm and methodically work your way up to the base of each finger. Use the thumb and forefinger to give the space between each finger a firm pinch and to pinch your way up to each fingertip. Finish by interlacing your fingers and extending your arms while turning the heels of your hands outward for 5 seconds.

- Squeeze a tennis ball or a handful of putty to work the cramps, knots, stiffness, and aches out of your hands. Most health product catalogs carry gadgets specifically for this.

- Clench your fingers into a tight fist, then fan them out. Repeat at least 6 times.

- Wrap a large rubber band around your fingers, then open and close them against the resistance.

- Bend back your wrist by pulling gently on your fingers. Hold for a count of 6.

▣ Start keeping a log of whatever stresses you out. This will help you become more conscious of which relationships and activities you ought to either prune back a bit or cut out entirely. Jot down when you develop headaches, shoulder or neck stiffness, burning stomach pain, acid indigestion, teeth clenching, and cheek bites. Remember to include the circumstances under which you tend to overeat or skip meals entirely.

▣ Space out meals so that you don't. Blood sugar is your body's major fuel, so keep it constant by eating regularly scheduled, more easily digestible small meals at even intervals throughout the day.

▣ If you must eat a big meal, chow down around 2:00 in the afternoon and eat a light supper before 8:00 at night.

⊠ Alcohol is a depressant that not only kills off brain cells and messes with your sleep cycle, but also slowly and surely leads to physiological and psychological addiction for a surprisingly large number of people. Find a healthier way to satisfy your desperate need to unwind.

⊠ You may nibble snacks or sip water at your desk, but do not eat lunch there. Just because you're working at home doesn't make this habit any healthier than it was at an outside-the-home office. Leave your office entirely or, at the very least, sit in your comfy chair and let your answering machine pick up your calls.

⊠ If you're under a lot of stress or feeling anxious, decrease the size and increase the frequency of your meals. When you're frazzled, your body thinks it needs to be ready to fight or flee. As a result, the blood you need to digest a large meal is transferred from your digestive tract to your arms and legs.

IN MY HUMBLE OPINION

It's a huge mistake to keep snacks in the office — and I mean that literally.

I used to keep cute little snacks in one of my file drawers. I figured miniature candy bars would take up less space and help me monitor intake. Wrong. Not only did I eat more than one, two, or, okay, a half-dozen bite-size anythings at one sitting, but I wasted a lot of time unwrapping them, too. As for small bags of munchies, I miscalculated there as well. Apparently, I need to crunch through at least three ounces before I get tired of chewing.

These days I'm saving my own life by not buying snacks with sugar or (obvious) salt to begin with. Whatever I do snack on, like cherry tomatoes and pickles, requires leaving my office. So I either end up forgetting about it or getting some exercise.

TOP STRESSORS	
• Poor time management	• Noise
• Overcommitment	• Competition and envy
• Multitasking	• Cranky, negative, demanding
• Clutter	people

⊞ Find a good massage therapist or other therapeutic body-workers who will make house calls for the price of the session plus travel time. While it's probably better to get the heck out of the office, having someone come to you is well worth the extra expense if you can:

• Schedule a session when no one else is around to distract you.

• Receive a massage in a room other than your office.

• Allow for at least 15 minutes of relaxation and integration time after the session before getting back to work.

• Resist racing from bodywork to desk.

Once you're familiar with the practitioner, arrange to pay in advance so the business transaction doesn't disturb your tranquillity.

Note: Massage therapists and therapeutic bodyworkers are health care providers and therefore should not be tipped over and above their standard fees.

HUMBLE OPINION

IN MY

Solo exercise is boring as hell. I'd almost rather be exhausted and fat than work out alone. If I can't get one of my working-from-home buddies to take a long walk with me, I watch television while I'm on the treadmill.

I find that sitcoms generally help release endorphins by providing a few laughs. If I really want to boost my heart rate, I watch the most insulting and enraging talk show I can find.

⊞ Relax by giving yourself a series of quick massages that don't require stripping down or slathering yourself with oil:

• Whip off your shoes and socks, then roll a golf ball all around the sole of your foot. Focus especially on the arch and the ridge between the base of your toes and the ball of your foot.

• Walk around barefoot as much as possible.

• With one hand on either side of your head, grab onto hanks of hair at the scalp and gently tug them in all directions for 5 seconds. Finish by pressing your thumbs into the base of your skull and giving yourself a vigorous scalp massage with your fingertips for another 5 seconds.

• Gently but firmly press along the upper ridge of your eyebrows with the forefingers of both hands. Work from the bridge of the nose to your temples, pressing each spot for 3 to 5 seconds. Finish by closing your eyes and pressing underneath the eyebrows close to the bridge of your nose for a few 5-second repetitions.

⊞ Schedule time for exercise and write it on your daily "To Do" list. The latest guideline for aerobic exercise is 30 minutes daily. But guess what — you don't have to do this all at once. You can do two 15-minute stints at different points of the day. Of course the benefit to exercising for at least 30 minutes at a time is that you're more likely to work up a good, dripping, toxin-releasing sweat.

- You've turned into a blob since you started working from home. You suspect your metabolism is changing, but maybe not. After trying a half-dozen of the trendiest diets, you've gained and lost a few tons. You're no longer sure what to eat and have run out of patience and energy. Go for a consultation with a nutritionist and don't just limit yourself to one trained in the "standard American diet." You may find that an ayurvedic practitioner or someone trained in traditional Chinese medicine may have some different, revealing, and helpful things to say about what and when you eat.

- Exercise makes you nauseous, or is it the fact that you've squandered hundreds of dollars on home exercise equipment over the years and use none of it? Consider hiring a personal trainer to come to your home, if only for a few sessions, to evaluate your needs and show you how to best use your existing equipment.

⊠ Get up and do something when:

- Your head is starting to swim and you can't concentrate.

- You catch yourself yawning or sighing a lot.

- You're in between big projects.

- You make three little bloopers or one whopping huge mistake.

> **"** If I need to clear my head, I pull on my shoes and go for a 40-minute run. If I don't, I'll get nothing done. I've learned that I start to procrastinate when I'm getting stuck in my work. To get unstuck, I have to remove myself from the work situation in a way that's active. For example, I wouldn't pick up a book. I take myself out for a run instead. **"**
>
> *Kitty,* **talent scout**

6 Producing a Professional Image

This may come as a total shock, but I must tell you that neatness does count, appearances aren't all that deceiving, and while looks may not be everything, they sure do help. Indeed, certain looks could kill — your business — if you don't watch out. Come on, admit it. Didn't that kid next door, the one with the really cool-looking lemonade stand, rope in more adults?

Back in chapter 3, I claimed you could operate a perfectly professional home office while wearing fuzzy slippers. I stand by that assertion — in slouch socks, as a matter of fact. However, this kind of unprofessional stuff works only if no one sees you and you do not *in any way* convey the image of someone who conducts business like a deadbeat.

In practical terms this means that anything and everything that puts you or your business before the public must be of top professional quality. Anything and everything of yours the public sees, hears, and touches must convey professionalism. Your business relationships and your business practices must convey professionalism. This is true for anyone who works from a home office and is doubly, especially true for anyone operating a home-based business.

Fortunately, professional images are not born, they're made. I know this because I was raised by parents who made me develop an impressively strong, steady handshake by puberty. You can learn business etiquette, get help creating a printed or graphic image, take a course in public speaking if need be, and re-record your outgoing message until it sounds — you guessed it — professional. In fact, I will go so far as to say that unless you commit to producing a professional image for you and your business, you'll either have a painfully short career or a long, torturous one. May the tips in this chapter support you in preventing either of these horrible options from coming to pass.

The attributes of professionalism are surprisingly congruent to those of adulthood, which may help explain why few people know how to behave like either. Before you can project a professional image, you have to know what one looks like. Then you have to act that way. Professionals:

- Combine a finely honed set of skills and talents with a realistic understanding of their limitations.
- Do what they say they're going to do.
- Appreciate the value of being on time, using time wisely, and notifying appropriate parties when time parameters need to be changed.
- Solve problems, rather than cause them.
- Are willing to be wrong, quick to admit not knowing, and gracious about apologizing when they behave like jerks.

⊠ Use your own name as your company name when you're selling a service and are already known in your field. Not only will this make it easier for clients and customers to find you, but it will also reinforce the fact that they're hiring a particular expert — you.

And because your own name is important, spring for the extra it costs for bold or boxed type in the telephone directory.

⊠ Wait as long as possible before designing a logo, or even choosing a company name if it's going to be something other than your own. These are essential aspects of your public image that you'll have to live with for years, and the process of creating an effective public identity takes time. Choose a name and logo prematurely and you may be saddled with something that ends up limiting you.

⊞ Not using your own name? That's perfectly okay, but avoid creating a name that:

- Starts with letters so far down the alphabet that no one will have the patience to slog through directory listings to find you. *(Note:* Telephone books aren't the only place to list your name and what you do. Investigate the available trade, professional, and business directories.)

- Is so cutesy, clever, or boring that it undermines your identity as a professional.

- Fails to adequately (or accurately) describe what you do or offer.

- You think is so fabulous that you don't test it in the marketplace. What you "like" will not necessarily resonate there.

⊞ Before announcing your new business name (and way before you print it anywhere), run a quick and thorough check to find out if anyone else has it or anything close enough to land you in hot legal water. (Also, check with state or local government to find out if you'll need to register a DBA — "doing business as" — or statement of fictitious business name if you're not using your own name.)

⊞ Business cards won't land you business, but a poorly designed and printed one can do you some damage. Trendy as it may be, avoid a business card with:

- Vertical designs that make it tough to read when placed in a business card file.

- Script or funky type, unless you're in a creative industry that tolerates that stuff. Even then, think twice about sticking yourself with a trendy print style.

- Long, descriptive lists of what you can do.

- Academic credentials, unless you're in an industry that's impressed by advanced degrees.

⊠ When you do enclose your business card (or give it away at a function), pass along three so the recipient has something to keep and something to pass on to someone else who might want your services.

⊠ Create a virtual business card by using a "signature file" to add an automatic footer to your e-mail messages. This can include your name, identify what you do and the industries you serve, and note how you may be reached by phone, by facsimile, and electronically.

⊠ Save administrative time by setting up accounts with major delivery and shipping services so you can receive forms with your name and account number preprinted on them. Save even more at your end by using customer account numbers for deliveries. In most cases, this establishes an accounting procedure they'll prefer without diminishing your professional image in the least.

⊠ Promote your services or products on-line first by introducing yourself in "new member" sections, then by developing an on-line presence. The quickest and most obvious way is by contributing to chat groups or special-interest forums. The operative word here is "contributing," which means being helpful, friendly, and forthcoming without being obviously self-serving. Save blatant horn blowing for on-line advertising.

⊠ Think twice before joining the burgeoning http://www world. Consider developing your own Web site if and only if you:

- Are sure that the customers and clients you want to reach are on-line.

- Have the design skills for this medium, or are willing to hire someone who does to design your Web page.

- Commit to finding the right list service, updating information on your Web site on a weekly basis and redesigning pages on a monthly basis, or are willing to hire a freelance Webmaster to do this.

- Plan to get statistics from your Web provider about what kinds of people actually visit your site, and follow up on them promptly — or are willing to hire someone who will.

⊠ Renting a post office box or one from a commercial mailing service serves several important functions. It:

- Protects your privacy by preventing customers from knowing your home address.

- Spares your residential mail carrier the burden of schlepping a large volume of business mail.

- May allow you to choose a more prestigious address.

- Keeps nosy neighbors in the dark about how much business you're actually doing from your home.

HUMBLE OPINION

IN MY

Most Web sites launch the visual equivalent of junk mail into an already-inundated world of junky communications. Call me retro, but I think clogging cyberspace with poorly executed images and badly written self-indulgent copy is not a good thing. The world would be much better served by freeing up the telephone lines to order take-out pizza.

⊠ Using the same font (type style) on everything establishes a continuity of image that makes a strong statement about your professionalism. Unless you hire a graphic designer who convinces you otherwise, limit yourself to no more than two compatible typefaces for your letterhead, envelopes, mailing labels, invoices, fax cover sheets, and business cards.

⊠ Get at least three bids from small commercial printers before using one of the fast-photocopy shops for offset printing. You may be surprised to find competitive prices and will receive better-quality printing and service. It doesn't matter whether you're printing one thousand business cards, reams of letterhead stationery, or hundreds of newsletters, make sure you have a contract that itemizes and prices:

• Type of paper stock.

• Ink color.

• Photo reproduction, screens, color separations.

• Proofing and corrections.

• Size of print run.

• Delivery date and penalties for delays.

⊠ If you're working with a graphic artist, it may be worth your while to have that professional deal directly with the printer. In this case, make sure you have a clear contract with the artist about handling printing, delivery, and delays.

⊞ Learn, then use, the language of phone etiquette at both ends of a phone conversation:

• "Thanks for returning my call."

• "Let me call you back when I have more time to listen."

• "Thanks for spending this time with me."

• "I appreciate your call."

• "I'll follow up on this, then get back to you."

⊞ Score more major good-impression points by:

• Returning all phone calls within one business day, even if you simply leave a voice mail message after regular business hours.

• Giving complete information in your phone message, including your phone number if you want a call-back.

• Giving explicit permission not to call you back if you don't need your call returned.

⊞ Answer your business phone with something more than "hello," such as your name, your company's name, a good-morning or good-afternoon greeting, or something equally pleasant.

⊞ Better communicating through technology:

• If you can't phone, send e-mail. If you can't send e-mail, send a short fax. If you can't send a short fax, send a letter or longer documents via overnight mail.

• When you send a fax, choose a typeface that will transmit crisply — something sans serif and slightly larger than your standard type size.

• See and hear yourself as others will: Fax a test document to yourself. Review both the content and tone of your phone answering message. Never use all caps in e-mail messages, unless, of course, you want to come off as SHOUTING.

- Keep all initial contacts short and simple: Leave succinct phone messages. Limit faxes to five pages (fewer if you can). Restrict yourself to a few short, pithy, clearly delineated paragraphs when you send e-mail.

- Make it easy for others to respond: Always include a call-back number when you leave a phone message. Program your fax machine to run phone and fax numbers on a header or footer, making sure to note which number is for what.

- Need information? Calling is your best bet. Giving information? Send an e-mail, fax, or letter.

- Create a subject line for your business e-mail that's clear. Save your incredibly clever, obscure double entendres for friends.

- Proofread everything you right. A spell checker won't catch homonyms.

⊞ "Do you have a minute?" If you do, by all means say "yes," but if you're squeezed for time, make sure callers know exactly how much time you can spare.

Conversely, do not ask anyone you're calling for a minute if you really need five. If you ask for five minutes and it looks like you'll need substantially longer, ask if it's okay to keep going, or whether it would be better to schedule another call. Your accuracy, honesty, and consideration will make a lasting good impression.

> ❝ I made the decision not to join professional associations because I realized I needed to get some distance from the whole industry scene. It can be so distracting. Even though I'm not as squarely in the network as some of my other colleagues, I think it's easier to preserve a unique individual perspective this way. ❞
>
> *Robin*, literary agent

Yes, you could generate this checklist yourself. Yes, you can find it in any book, magazine article, or newspaper column about home offices. And yes, here it is again.

Joining at least one organization in each of the following categories will not only provide an arena to promote whatever it is you do from your home office, but will also keep you from becoming too isolated from other sentient beings.

Plan to become a dues-paying member (for the newsletter and other perks), if not a regular attendee, at:

- Local professional or trade associations (e.g., chamber of commerce, Kiwanis Club, Rotary, Lions). Remember to check out networking groups organized around any of your special interests or statuses.
- National professional and trade associations. In addition to joining ones that will help you stay current in your field, consider joining ones in a marketing niche you'd like to develop.
- Alumni associations for your undergraduate college, trade school, graduate school, and Greek letter societies.
- On-line chat groups or special-interest forums in your area of expertise, as well as for home office workers.

If you've joined one or some of these organizations, attended a few functions, and still believe your particular needs aren't being met, consider starting your own support group. You may find that a heterogenous group of home-based office workers will share more practical concerns than a homogenous group of industry-specific colleagues.

To find similarly situated others, think about the pit stops along your errand route — office supply stores, photocopy shops, public libraries, and java joints. These are the best places to post notices and announcements that will be seen by other home-based entrepreneurs.

Treating competitors as adversaries rather than colleagues is a big mistake. In my experience, there ain't no such thing as total congruence among so-called competitors. Even if the services offered are exactly the same, styles will differ sufficiently to make sharing worth everyone's while.

Some of my best leads and referrals have come from competitors. In exchange, I've happily off-loaded clients who were grating on my nerves. After all, one person's dream client is another person's nightmare.

In addition, I believe that every business or industry has at least one common enemy that each competitor has to deal with — regulatory agencies, overzealous community groups, suppliers from hell — so why not join forces over that?

⊠ Be prepared to give an on-the-spot interview anytime you make a cold call, or one to follow up a promotional letter. Before dialing the phone, haul out your cover letter and résumé. Generate a written set of points you want to pitch, then remember to use them.

⊠ A short, written thank-you note conveys maturity, goodwill, and human decency. You will distinguish yourself among colleagues and competitors alike if you get into this habit.

⊠ Chances are better than average that the editor of your alumni association magazine is always looking for stories about successful graduates. Do not hesitate to pitch one about what you're doing from your home office if, objectively speaking, it'll be inspiring or interesting to other graduates.

And don't forget to send short blurbs about what you're up to for the "class notes" section.

⊞ Be careful to strike a balance between developing a presence and becoming overinvolved in professional associations. When starting out:

- Attend four to six meetings before deciding whether the organization is a good one for you.

- Plan in advance what to say when asked to introduce yourself as a new member.

- Be strategic in your contribution to group discussions, especially at business meetings. Wait until you understand the culture before offering your breathtakingly valuable insights. Participate in question-and-answer sessions only if you have an authentically interesting question to ask.

- Resist all temptations to volunteer for anything during your first few months of attendance. Don't let burned-out members drain your new blood.

- Watch your calendar. The organizations may only meet once a month, but if you're attending a slew of them you may book yourself into meetings weekly or more often.

⊞ Get used to writing thank-you notes. These don't have to be frilly handwritten missives on pretty paper, they just have to be prompt acknowledgments of:

- Information requested or received.

- Business bought.

- Interviews granted.

- Seminars, workshops, articles, or anything attended or read of special value.

⊞ No major business would seriously consider plowing ahead without the advice and consent of a board of directors. While you may not want or need consent, getting regular advice is prudent if you're starting a new business of your own.

Enhance your ability to see what you're doing more clearly by:

- Creating an advisory board. This can be a group of colleagues who meet regularly to give you feedback, or a more informal network of contacts whom you call on a regular basis for industry-specific reality checks.

- Inviting a group of trusted friends to review your goals periodically. These people don't have to be in your line of work to target potential problems such as overcommitting and overworking. You might, in fact, consider asking them to focus exclusively on your work processes.

- Sitting yourself down for regular meetings during which you review goals, note accomplishments, and plan for the next quarter or year.

⊞ When creating a marketing communications plan, keep in mind that getting media publicity about who you are, what you do, and what you think is almost always more cost-effective than placing an advertisement. Here's why:

- Everyone knows advertising is paid for by the advertiser. Articles in newspapers and magazines, or mentions on talk shows, are almost never perceived as being placed, even though the vast majority of what shows up as news has indeed been placed by a paid publicist.

- Editors and producers are always in the market for information, news, and stories. These days, stories about independent entrepreneurs, home-based office workers, and small businesses are perceived as being of particular interest to readers, listeners, and viewers.

⊞ Personally addressed mail is often treated more seriously and carefully than mail that is simply sent to the "business editor."

⊞ Before defining specific strategies and tactics for your marketing communications plan, ask (and answer!) the following questions:

- Who is my audience and where will I find them?

- What do I want to tell them and how can I best communicate to them?

- How do I want them to respond and what do I want them to do?

⊞ Send press releases to announce events, services, activities, or commendations directly to whomever is in charge of reviewing these things. Generally speaking, if the news is business related, it goes to the business editor. If it's of more general human interest, it may go to the lifestyle editor. One quick phone call to the switchboard operator of the publication should yield the right contact name.

⊞ Limit press releases to one page of double-spaced typed text. Sometimes you can get away with submitting a fact sheet rather than a narrative. You may include more extensive information (e.g., a backgrounder about your company) if

> **"** Just because we work together from our home office every day doesn't mean we have time to do long-range planning. We figure if we were still with outside companies we'd be going on regular off-site planning retreats, and so three times a year we hold one for ourselves.
>
> We get rooms at a retreat center or affordable health spa where we can relax after planning sessions. We arrive equipped with flip chart paper, markers, tape recorders, laptop computers, and whatever we need to be productive. Before we leave our home office, we agree on a theme for that particular retreat. So far we've gone off-site to do long-range planning, reconfigure our office procedures, and reevaluate our market. **"**
>
> *Len and Phyllis,* **mail-order sales**

you honestly think your news rates more than a paragraph in the "people in the news" column.

Unless your press release is really boring or poorly written, submitting a good quality photograph with it will enhance your chances of anything getting printed.

⊞ Press releases are edited from the bottom up, so make sure all your vital information is covered in the first paragraph. In other words, you want your release to make sense even if the last two paragraphs are hacked off to save space.

⊞ Just one mention in the right newspaper or magazine at the right time can generate massive numbers of inquiries. Make sure you're prepared to handle them.

⊞ Check the reference section of your local library for copies of standard media guides such as *Bacon's Publicity Checker, Broadcasting Yearbook, Gale Directory of Publications,* and *Hudson's Newsletter Directory.*

⊞ You may call journalists, reporters, and newspaper editors directly. Some, in fact, prefer a phone pitch if the story you have involves time-bound news. But make your phone contact snappy, conveying your idea in a concise sentence or two.

Self-serving stories about you and your business won't fly, so don't even try to launch them. Instead, focus on a newsworthy trend in your business or industry that you can expertly blather on about.

⊞ Propose your story in writing if it's too complex to pitch on the phone, it's "evergreen" (can be written and published at any time), or you simply communicate better in writing. A simple personal letter to an individual editor is fine. Go ahead and use bullet points if you're suggesting an article idea and offering yourself as expert resource. Your letter will need to demonstrate writing ability and you'll need to include a few clips of published work if you're proposing yourself as the writer.

⊠ Consider publishing a quarterly newsletter to use as a sales tool. Keep it short, simple, and focused. You can focus on what's going on in:

- Your business or industry. This type of newsletter provides handy tips and information. You will come to be perceived as a player, someone who knows what's happening. Stay away from fluff.

- Your head. This type of newsletter gives readers a few minutes, in print, of your time and expertise. Stay away from self-aggrandizing hype.

⊠ Go ahead and launch an advertising campaign if and only if you are willing to:

- Hire an experienced copywriter to create the copy. You can noodle around with a rough draft or copy points, but let someone who knows how to do this special kind of persuasive writing come up with whatever finally goes to press.

- Spend whatever is necessary to buy good writing, strong design, and decent media space.

- Maintain a continuous presence in print for at least one year without whimpering about not seeing results. Not that you won't see results from your advertising within a year —just don't count on it, especially not if you're trying to sell a service. What you can count on is looking like a flake if your ad periodically appears and disappears from print.

- Respond promptly to whatever inquiries your ad generates.

⊠ If public speaking is your thing, enhance your professional visibility by developing and giving short talks in front of business, community, and professional organizations. These groups are always looking for good breakfast and luncheon speakers. Contact whomever is chairing the program committee to find out which topics they've already covered and which ones they'd like to address.

Please don't say "advertising" when you mean "public rela-tions," or "marketing" when you mean "advertising." These are distinct disciplines that involve different types of activities and are used strategically to accomplish different goals.

Marketing generally refers to the process of identifying the needs and wants of the marketplace. You simply cannot intelli-gently bring a product or a service to market without knowing if anyone will bother to notice, let alone buy it. You must under-stand the market — the one that already exists, or the one you plan to create. (By the way, there are precious few aspects of mar-keting that cannot be orchestrated and done, at least in part, from a home office.)

So now you have your product or service. Preliminary research indicates that it'll be well received. You know *who* needs to know about it. Now you have to get the news and information out there. This is where marketing communications — advertising and public relations — come in.

Advertising is paid communication through various media. It's a controlled way of placing a message before a public. Readers, viewers, and listeners know darn well that the advertiser has created the ad and paid handsomely for space or on-air time. And there are many different types of ads: classified, display, box, radio and tele-vision spots, billboards, and posters at bus stops, for example.

Public relations is another form of persuasion, directed at tar-geted publics. Public relations activities also deliver a message, but not necessarily (or exclusively) through print and electronic media. Public relations tactics certainly include other efforts such as special events, contests, trade shows, lobbying, community relations, and promotions. The messages delivered through these tactics are generally perceived as infinitely more credible than advertising, because they look like they appear out of the blue, for free. But it requires creative imagination and effort to execute suc-cessful public relations activities. If you want to see grown public relations people weep, refer to their work as "free advertising."

- You've decided to publish a newsletter and you're a pretty good writer, but you're not visual and your brain crashes in the presence of desktop publishing programs. Hire a graphic designer who can organize your material visually and help you with illustrations.

- You're a genius in your field — everyone says. Unfortunately, you don't come across so great in public. You have trouble conveying what you do, then get irritated when people ask questions. Or you think talking about your work is a form of selling, which you perceive as bad. Clients like your work, but can't stand dealing with you. Find someone who can competently and professionally represent you and your work.

- You travel a lot for business. A lot. You could go on-line and make your own plane reservations, but that seems to take up more time than you have to spare. Hook up with a good travel agent, one who understands business travel, and let that person handle all your transportation arrangements.

◈ Whenever you do any public speaking, remember to:

- Publicize your talk in advance. If the group doesn't routinely post this information in the local paper, ask if they'd mind your doing so.

- Get permission to display brochures, information sheets, and any other printed materials you may have about yourself and what you do.

- Bring along a hefty number of business cards and do not hesitate to hand them out.

⊞ If possible, arrange to meet clients or customers in person to see their operations, meet their employees, review their needs, and check out the chemistry before committing to a final price quote. This also gives them an opportunity to look you over.

⊞ Keep notes about any quirky habits, preferences, or dislikes your customers may have to help you serve them better. Do whatever you have to do to remember names and the correct spelling of them.

⊞ Handle complaints calmly and quickly by listening carefully to the whole tale without interrupting, taking accurate notes, and resisting any urge to fight fire with fire.

Give yourself time to completely assess the situation before taking any action on complaints. You should, however, promise to take action and give your customer a time by which you will follow up. Keep this promise, even if the answer is going to start another round of complaints.

⊞ Just because you're working from a home office doesn't mean you can junk your résumé. You may still need it, but you'll need to reformat it to reflect your current status and office capabilities. Consider turning your formal résumé into a one-page work biography.

7

CHAPTER

Establishing the Business of Business

S ome people have absolutely no problem with the business of business. They view getting licenses and permits as an adventure, happily noodle around with the latest spreadsheet software, boldly set prices, and are fearless when it comes to dealing with government agencies such as the Internal Revenue Service. Others immediately break out in a cold sweat at the slightest suggestion of anything legal or financial. Far be it from me to make any gross generalizations — even though I have a terminal degree in sociology — but I've noticed that mental health professionals, creative types, and healing arts practitioners tend to freak out over routine business practices. Not that management consultants, bookkeepers, or financial planners win any awards for diligence. All of which just proves the old adage that the cobbler's kids have no shoes.

So what's my point?

I guess it's that the business of business requires some work, regardless of anyone's particular skill set.

This chapter's tips cover the nitty-gritty, necessary details of doing a business from a home office. Like the chapter about equipment, this one covers the basics. A more detailed exposition of the nuances of business development, tax accounting, pension planning, and pricing is way beyond the scope of this book or the tolerance of its author.

⊠ Check local zoning ordinances before getting your business up and running. One quick call to the local chamber of commerce should help you identify which board or planning commission to call. Resist the urge to launch into a long story about your fabulous new business. Simply ask to be sent information about zoning laws.

⊠ You generally have nothing to worry about if you operate a one-person business out of your home. You may, however, run into a snag if you have employees wandering in and out, or your business generates traffic or parking problems, especially in a residential area.

⊠ Without the proper permits, things could get really dicey if you're doing anything that annoys your neighbors (e.g., generating pollution or noise; building separate client entrances; hanging out a shingle; storing materials in your yard).

⊠ While you're on the phone, call the Department of Labor or Secretary of State's office to find out if your business violates any state laws regulating home-based work. This call is an absolute must if you're planning to manufacture, produce — or cook — anything out of your home.

⊠ If you live in a condominium or cooperative apartment building, check the by-laws to make sure you're not violating any of them. Don't like the rules? Check with an attorney to find out if they're truly legal. The rules may even be unconstitutional, a thrilling prospect for the slightly litigious.

⊠ Gather all the conventional wisdom you can about your proposed business, then ask colleagues, friends, and customers to tell you about their real live experiences. You may find that "conventional wisdom" does not account for your special situation or circumstances. Pay proper obeisance to your gut instincts if you've been in the field for a chunk of time.

⊞ Before you start writing a business plan, set aside a period of time to generate a personal vision. Eventually you'll want to put this into a statement, but don't worry about that as you start the process. Imagine the best of all possible work worlds without limiting yourself to such mundane dimensions as time, age, money, and other resources. Ask yourself questions about what will bring a sense of accomplishment, pride, joy, usefulness, integrity, and comfort to you in your own skin. Using whatever works best for you — writing, drawing, babbling into a tape recorder — express what you want to do, who you want to be, and how you want to work. The overlap between dreams and reality is greater than you might suspect.

Put yourself through this exercise again before you set up your home office. Where do you want it to be? What do you want it to look like? How do you want to feel while you're in there? What would help you accomplish that?

⊞ Start, but don't limit yourself to local bankers for start-up (or expansion) funding. Take time to investigate what's available through:

• The Small Business Administration, which has everything from Microloans for $25,000 to 80% guaranteed loans as hefty as $750,000.

• Nonbank lenders, such as venture capitalists who are keen on entrepreneurs, small business investment companies that specialize in long-term loans, and operating units of major credit card and brokerage houses developed especially for this purpose.

• Friends, family, and professional associates, such as doctors, dentists, lawyers, and accountants.

⊞ Choose a legal form for your business that best suits what you do and how you do it, your tax position, your liability status, and any other legal obligations you may have (e.g., support payments). Your options include: sole proprietorship, independent contractor, corporation, and partnership. Unless there are clear, quantifiable reasons to do otherwise, start out as simply as possible.

You'll need to take most, if not all, of these steps on the road to a successful home-based business. The first four items on this list must pave the way. After them, you can probably get away with a few detours.

1. Research your market: Does anyone need or want what you have to sell? Can you create a need or want if one doesn't exist? Can you ride the wave of an incoming trend? Who's your competition? How are they doing?
2. Investigate zoning, licenses, and permits: Will you be able to do the work you want to do from your home?
3. Write a business plan: Describe your business; profile your customer base; outline your marketing plan; estimate start-up costs, operating expenses, and projected income.
4. Secure funding: Will you need to go to a lender or do you have the bucks to get up and running?
5. Open a business bank account.
6. Set up systems for financial accounting and time management.
7. Purchase equipment and supplies.
8. Buy property, liability, health, and disability insurance.
9. Set up your office space.
10. Register your business name.
11. Register to pay sales tax.
12. Implement your marketing plan.

⊠ Reduce the cost of health care coverage by:

- Finding and enrolling in a decent HMO ("health maintenance organization") or PPO ("paid provider organization").

- Increasing your deductible to a thousand dollars and choosing a 60/40 copayment if you don't want to go the HMO or PPO route.

- Paying premiums in larger chunks (e.g., semiannually) rather than monthly to lock in the rate.

- Buying a plan with a large pool of insured so that rate increases aren't astronomical and your claims don't skew the numbers. Compare what's available through your chamber of commerce, professional or trade association, fraternal organization, or college alumni group.

- Focusing on wellness and preventative medicine. Study what holistic practitioners say about the body/mind connection; collect information about the therapeutic use of vitamins and herbs; get and stay healthy with a proper diet and regular exercise.

⊠ Product or service liability insurance? Don't stay home without it if there's even a remote chance that whatever you do/make/offer might injure someone.

Because they're specific to your enterprise, professional or trade associations may offer exactly the type of product or service liability coverage you need. Otherwise, consult with your insurance agent.

⊠ When shopping for insurance, look for an independent agent who represents a number of companies rather than someone employed by any one insurer. An independent agent will be better able to mix and match policies to provide the coverage you need. Your best bet is someone who understands the needs and requirements of home-based business owners.

The safe should, of course, be easily accessible, fireproof, and floodproof.

- Bank account and credit card information
- Equipment inventory: place and date of purchase, serial number, price and sales receipt, photograph/video of all assets, warranties
- Insurance policies: agent's name and number, expiration date
- Legal documents: deeds, titles, lease agreements, certifications, articles of incorporation, stocks, savings bonds, securities
- Lists of assets and liabilities, plus one of who owes you what along with documentary proof

⊠ Add a rider to your existing homeowner's policy to cover the contents of your office. Buy enough property insurance to cover the cost of replacing equipment, furnishings, supplies, and inventory. Make sure your policy adjusts automatically for inflation.

If your current insurer won't allow you to add a rider, shop around before buying a separate business owner's policy.

⊠ Remember to include liability coverage that not only protects clients and customers who visit your home office, but also protects you when you work off your home site.

⊠ Keep a separate credit card for business. This will help at tax time, because many of your deductible items will be in one place. If you'd rather use "cash," always get receipts or pay by check so you have proper documentation for expenses.

⊠ Order regular credit reports for yourself to see how your credit rating will appear to others. Check the credit references of clients and customers by contacting their previous creditors by phone or in writing.

⊠ Either keep personal and business accounts totally separate, or keep fanatically detailed records of what was spent, when it was spent, and why.

⊠ Your social security number can serve as the federal ID number for your business. If you want a separate employer identification number (even if you have no employees), you will need to file Form SS-4 with the Internal Revenue Service. By the way, getting one of these numbers is one of the little, easy ways to present a more professional image.

⊠ Stash a business mileage log in your car and jot pertinent information down before turning on the engine. At minimum you'll need to record the date, your destination, and your total number of miles.

If you want or need to be more precise, note where you're traveling from and where you'll be going. Developing a code for regular trips will make it easier to record this information.

⊠ Create a monthly folder or separate envelope into which you put receipts, canceled checks, credit card statements, and other expense documents throughout the month. At the end of each month, set aside time to sort and organize this information chronologically so you can more accurately calculate your estimated quarterly taxes.

Make it even easier on yourself by keeping a separate envelope for whatever you can submit to clients for expense reimbursement.

⊠ Choose a financial record-keeping system that suits your learning style. If you're primarily kinesthetic, tapping numbers into a calculator and writing tallies down in pencil will work well for you. If you're primarily visual, computer software programs will be fine. You'll know the system is wrong for you if you consistently find yourself feeling burdened and frustrated by the complexity of this relatively simple bookkeeping task.

▨ Business accounting software is not the same as tax-preparation software. Hack around with tax-preparation software if you must, but unless you're well versed in the ever-changing, convoluted tax rules, hire a bona fide tax accountant to do the dirty work.

WHAT TO KEEP AND WHAT TO TOSS

Keep:
- Back tax records for at least six years — longer if you have capital gains you're carrying forward, have investment losses, or are making contributions to a nondeductible Individual Retirement Account.
- Checking account statements and the canceled checks and receipts you need for tax purposes, for six years.
- Credit card statements for at least six months, unless you need to document tax deductions.
- All retirement plan documents and annual statements.
- Investment materials, including statements, prospectuses, brokerage agreements, and trade confirmations.

Toss:
- Deposit slips after the deposits show up on your monthly statement.
- Canceled checks for stuff that isn't tax deductible.
- Old insurance policies when updates arrive and until the statute of limitations runs out on the expired policy.

⊟ How much money do you need to make a year? How does that break down by month? By week? By hour? Write this up and post it where you can see it every day. It'll turn to wallpaper soon, but by then the subliminal power of the message will be embedded in your brain.

⊟ Protect yourself against seasonal (or other) fluctuations in income by cultivating a variety of income streams. In practical terms, this means cultivating a broad client base, one that includes repeat clients; continually casting your net for business prospects and following up on leads; and earning income from other sources such as writing, teaching, or consulting.

> **66** To determine how much money I had to make, I began by looking at my bills and what I needed to cover them. I added in a surplus, then worked out an hourly rate from that.
>
> Of course *knowing* how much money you need and *getting* that much money are two different things. It's the biggest frustration I have and I know I am not alone. All the experts say, 'Don't dwell on the money — provide a good service or product and the money will follow.' That may be true for someone out there, but I've found that getting the money to follow takes a lot of hard work. **99**
>
> *Mike,* **patent agent**

⊟ Understand the difference between billable time (what they're paying you to do) and nonbillable time (what you need to do to stay in business). It's perfectly okay to charge clients for the proportion of administrative time that you spend on their account. The rest of the time you spend futzing around with your business you'll have to eat. Still, you can account for it when pricing your professional services.

⊟ Your rate should also include a percentage increase for:

• Rush jobs.

• Client changes after a certain point in the process.

Ego, pride, and certain hormonal configurations distort most people's perceptions of how much they have to make. I thought I had to make as much as (if not more than) what I made at the company I left. Then I made myself complete a reality-check exercise.

I made a list of all my living expenses, including the frippery I was unwilling to give up — like facials every six months — then took a good look at the bottom line. I was shocked, then thrilled and very relieved to discover that what I actually needed to earn was significantly lower than what my terrified lower self demanded I rake in. Getting real really helped me make a more comfortable transition to working from home.

- Running hither and thither, especially if thither is far away.

- Late payments.

⊞ When you're asked to submit a project estimate or bid, remember to increase whatever price you come up with by 15 to 20 percent to cover unforeseen weird stuff. Uh, you'll want to add that percentage *before* you submit your bid.

⊞ Track all your time — including personal activities — even if you're charging on a per-project basis. Doing this faithfully will help you:

- Submit accurate bills for your services. (Research actually shows that the more accurate the records, the higher the income.)

- More accurately estimate the time and price of similar jobs/projects in the future.

- See how much time you're squandering on nonbillable personal activities.

- Generate detailed status reports to submit with invoices.

Only fools or those with incredibly low self-esteem underprice their services. People really believe the adage, "you get what you pay for" and find low rates suspect. It seems counterintuitive, but more often than not, underpricing decreases the quantity of clients and customers.

I also happen to think you get what you price for. Is it my imagination, or are the bargain-hunting, cheapskate clients more annoying than those who are willing to spend a buck? I noticed a definite improvement in client quality when I raised my rates.

▣ Tailor the style of your price quote to the work culture of your customer. Corporate clients won't wince at per diem rates and may, in fact, dismiss you as bush league if you trot out an hourly rate. Small businesses, however, generally plotz when they hear the words "per diem," preferring to pay by the hour even if the hours total up to — you guessed it — your day rate.

▣ It may be to your economic and psychological advantage to quote a fixed project price irrespective of client wealth. If you work smart, you stand a better chance of making a profit while they bask in the knowledge that you won't gut their budget.

▣ Remember to account for the OOPs ("out-of-pocket expenses") when you draw up your letter of agreement. These are expenses for which you'll get reimbursed at cost — telephone, photocopying, delivery services, travel, lodging, meals, and the like. They should be billed separately, with the appropriate documentation provided. You can, of course, simply quote a project price, but you'll probably end up losing money unless you excel at estimates. If you decide to go the latter route, do so with smaller clients. Larger, corporate clients expect the former type of billing.

▣ Consider pricing your service so that you get a certain amount immediately to cover your costs, plus a cut of whatever your clients earn in the future as a result of your work. For this to work, you'll need to have a very clear, written agreement that includes how the positive impact of your contribution will be measured.

▣ Start efforts to collect the money due you if you do not get paid within 30 days. First, call accounts payable to make sure they have the paperwork approving payment from your client contact. If they don't have that paperwork, call your client's assistant to find out if it's still languishing on a desk somewhere. In other words, don't bug clients or customers directly until you've established that they haven't signed off on the invoice.

▣ Once you've established that your bill is in accounts payable, feel free to be a persistent but pleasant pest. You're allowed to become a little less pleasant if they string you along for more than 60 days.

At that point, seriously consider turning the whole thing over to a collection agency, attorney, or friend with more moxie than you if big bucks are involved.

▣ When you land clients or customers, immediately send a letter thanking them for their business and documenting any preliminary agreements you've made about the work, deadlines, fees, and payment terms. Follow up within a week with a formal contract or letter of agreement that everyone signs before starting work.

▣ Set up a billing file and fill out as much as the invoice as you can when you land a client. This will make it easier to bill promptly.

Ah, clients and customers. They're the ones who make it possible for you to work from the cozy confines of your home office. Some are your daily Wonder Bread, truly helping you build business in many terrific ways. Others literally make you choke with aggravation.

These are the P.I.T.A. ("pain in the ass") clients. They made your life miserable when you worked for someone else and will do the same now that you're on your own. But the difference between P.I.T.A. clients out there and those in your own client base is that now you get to bill them for the havoc they wreak. Feel free to gleefully (and secretly) charge extra for any of the following client misbehavior:

- Calling on weekends or at ridiculous hours when normal human beings are sleeping. Charge extra-extra if they use your beeper for nonessential stuff during national holidays.
- Telling you it's a super-rush job, then delaying feedback for weeks claiming internal review problems.
- Becoming instant experts in what they've hired you to do. Suddenly they're multitalented writers, award-winning artists, computer systems wizards, financial geniuses, and marketing gurus.
- Revising the specs midway through the project for everything you've already suggested or produced.
- Demanding you drop everything and everyone for their project, then neglecting to give you the input you need on time. Charge extra-extra if this essential input arrives at 4:45 p.m. on a Friday.
- Asking for your counsel, ignoring it, then going berserk when what they've decided to do instead doesn't work.
- Being abusive in the form of blaming, whining, cursing, or wasting your time with really lame jokes that you already heard from your 12-year-old.

Each month . . .
- Send out invoices.
- Pay bills.
- Review and balance your bank accounts.
- Summarize business expenses.
- Record business income.
- Restock office supplies as needed.
- Check and restock inventory as necessary.

End of year . . .
- Create new records files, folders, or envelopes.
- Set aside all tax-preparation documents.
- Review your income and expenses.
- Create a new budget.
- Run and review your projections sheet to evaluate how to increase profits and decrease expenses.
- Update resource lists, names, and addresses.

⊞ Client conference reports are a handy way to keep on task. Use these memos to document when you met, who attended, and what you agreed to do by when. When P.I.T.A. clients are involved, send a copy to them that ends with "Unless I hear from you in five business days, I will assume this aligns with your understanding and will proceed."

- Numbers make you woozy, you hate balancing your personal checkbook, you barely have time to do your work let alone punch numbers into anything allegedly helpful, and you're firmly convinced that you were born without left-brain functioning. Farm out your bookkeeping to a book-keeper, your financial management to an accountant, and your taxes to a tax-preparation professional.

- You think you might want to incorporate, friends think you're being ripped off, and you're generally paranoid (except you call it cautious and prudent) about business dealings. You skipped business law in undergraduate school and never understood a word of what went on during episodes of *L.A. Law* (or *Perry Mason*, for that matter). Hire an attorney to answer your legal questions and handle your legal affairs.

- Live presentations are your forte. You've got the gift of gab. An admirer once said you could sell someone his own dirty underwear and convince him that he got a deal. Alas, you cannot write a sentence that makes sense, let alone a whole proposal or business plan. Hire a consultant who specializes in this kind of writing, someone who can put your great ideas and potential contribution into words.

Recommended Reading

Bolles, Richard Nelson. *What Color Is Your Parachute?* Berkeley, CA: Ten Speed Press, 1996.

Burns, David D. *Feeling Good: The New Mood Therapy.* New York: William Morrow and Company, Inc., 1980.

Butler, Sharon. *Conquering Carpal Tunnel Syndrome.* Berwyn, PA: Advanced Press, 1995.

Cameron, Julia, with Mark Bryan. *The Artist's Way.* New York: Jeremy P. Tarcher/Putnam, 1992.

Dodt, Colleen K. *The Essential Oils Book.* Pownal, VT: Storey Communications, Inc., 1996.

Edwards, Paul, and Sarah Edwards. *Working from Home.* Los Angeles: Jeremy P. Tarcher, Inc., 1990.

Fisher, Roger, and William Ury. *Getting to Yes: Negotiating Agreement without Giving In.* New York: Penguin Books, 1981.

Ford-Grabowsky, Mary (editor). *Prayers for All People.* New York: Doubleday, 1995.

Frohbieter-Mueller, Jo. *Stay Home and Mind Your Own Business.* White Hall, VA: Betterway Publications, Inc., 1987.

Holtz, Herman. *The Complete Work-at-Home Companion.* Rocklin, CA: Prima Publishing, 1994.

Jeffers, Susan. *Feel the Fear and Do It Anyway.* New York: Fawcett Columbine, 1987.

Knaster, Mirka. *Discovering the Body's Wisdom.* New York: Bantam Books, 1996.

Lockwood, Georgene. *The Complete Idiot's Guide to Organizing Your Life.* New York: Alpha Books, 1996.

Marrs, Donald. *Executive in Passage.* Los Angeles: Barrington Sky Publishing, 1990.

Palmer, Helen. *The Enneagram in Love and Work.* San Francisco: HarperSan Francisco, 1995.

Shimer, Porter. *Keeping Fitness Simple.* Pownal, VT: Storey Communications, Inc., 1998.

von Oech, Roger. *A Whack on the Side of the Head.* New York: Warner Books, 1983.

Wong, Eva. *Feng Shui: The Ancient Wisdom of Harmonious Living for Modern Times.* Boston: Shambala Press, 1996.

Organizations

This directory lists national organizations that support people in small businesses. Some of these organizations offer education information, contacts, and resources. Others provide benefits such as group insurance rates and product discounts. Many of these business resource organizations offer information free of charge — but be sure to check.

American Business
 Women's Association
9100 Ward Parkway, Box 8728
Kansas City, MO 64114
phone: 816-361-6621
fax: 816-361-4991
e-mail: abwa@abwahq.org
website: http://www.abwahq.org

American Entrepreneurs
 Association
7501 Highway 290 East
Austin, TX 78723
phone: 512-933-1983
fax: 512-0933-1984
e-mail: triplett@grow_biz.com
website: http://www.grow_biz.com

American Institute of Small
 Business
7515 Wayzata Boulevard, Suite 201
Minneapolis, MN 55426
phone: 800-328-2906 or
 612-545-7001
fax: 612-545-7020
e-mail: aisbofmn@aol.com
website: http://www.acessil.com

American Management Association
135 W. 50th Street
New York, NY 10020
phone: 212-586-8100

American Marketing Association
2505 S. Wacker Drive, Suite 200
Chicago, IL 60606
phone: 312-648-0536

American Small Business
 Association
720 Seventh Street NW, Suite 304
Washington, DC 20001-3716
phone: 800-474-6340
fax: 202-639-0999
e-mail: asba@mnsinc.com
website: http://www.asba.net

Association of Shareware
 Professionals
5437 Honey Manor Drive
Indianapolis, IN 46221
phone: 317-856-6092
website: http://www.asp.
 shareware.org

Association of Small Business
Development Centers
1313 Farnam, Suite 132
Omaha, NE 68182
phone: 402-595-2387

Council of Better Business
Bureaus
1515 Wilson Boulevard
Arlington, VA 22209
phone: 703-276-0100

Entrepreneurship Institute
3592 Corporate Dr., Suite 101
Columbus, OH 43231
phone: 614-895-1153

Equipment Leasing Association
1300 North Seventeenth Street
Arlington, VA 22209
phone: 703-527-8655

Health Insurance Association
of America
1025 Connecticut Ave., NW,
Suite 1200
Washington, DC 20036
phone: 202-824-1600

Insurance Information Institute
110 Williams Street
New York, NY 10038
phone: 212-669-9200

National Alliance of Business
1201 New York Ave., NW,
Suite 700
Washington, DC 20005
phone: 202-289-2888

National Association for Business
Organizations
P.O. Box 30149
Baltimore, MD 21270
phone: 410-876-0502

National Association for Female
Executives
135 West 50th Street, 16th floor
New York, NY 10020
phone: 212-445-6235
e-mail: nafe@nafe.com

National Association of
Professional Organizers
P.O. Box 880656
San Diego, CA 92168
phone: 619- 687-7207

National Association for
the Self-Employed (NASE)
2328 Gravel Road
Ft. Worth, TX 76118
phone: 800-827-9990
website: http://www.
selfemployed.nase.org/NASE

National Association of Women
Business Owners (NAWBO)
600 S. Federal Street, Suite 400
Chicago, IL 60605
phone: 312-322-0990

National Federation of
Independent Business (NFIB)
600 Maryland Ave., SW., Suite 700
Washington, DC 20024-2567
phone: 202-554-9000

National Small Business
  Association
1604 K. Street, NW
Washington, DC 20006
phone: 202-293-8830

National Small Business United
1155 15th Street, NW, Suite 710
Washington, DC 20005
phone: 202-293-8830

Service Corps of Retired Executives
  (SCORE)
1825 Connecticut Avenue, NW,
  Suite 503
Washington, DC 20009
phone: 202-205-6762

Small Business Assistance Center
P.O. Box 1441
Worcester, MA 01601
phone: 508-756-3513

Small Business Network
P.O. Box 30149
Baltimore, MD 21270
phone: 410-581-1373

Small Business Service Bureau
554 Main Street., Box 1441
Worcester, MA 01601-1441
phone: 508-756-3513

Small Business Support Center
  Association
8811 Westheimer Road, #210
Houston, TX 77063-3617
phone: 713-773-6500

Support Services Alliance
P.O. Box 130
Schoharie, NY 12157
phone: 518-295-7966

U.S. Chamber of Commerce
1615 H. Street, NW
Washington, DC 20062
phone: 800-638-6582 or
  202-659-6000

U.S. Department of Labor
200 Constitution Avenue, NW
Washington, DC 20210
phone: 202-219-6666

U.S. Department of the Treasury
Internal Revenue Service
P.O. Box 25866
Richmond, VA 23289
phone: 800-829-3676 or
  202-566-2041

U.S. Small Business Administration
  (SBA)
1441 L Street, NW
Washington, DC 20062
phone: 716-282-4612

Index

Page numbers in *italic* indicate illustrations.

E-mail (continued)
  "signature file" for, 115
  sorting and filing, 57
Employer identification number, 136
Employers
  clients and customers of, 81
  as clients or customers, 75
  and telecommuting, 76–78, 81
Environment. *See* Work space
Equipment. *See also specific pieces*
  budget for, 27, 32
  buying, 27, 31, 35, 37
  and ergonomics, 44, 104, 105
  getting rid of, 32
  leasing, 33
  multipurpose, 33
  placement of, 22–23, 38
  returning, 37
  service agreements for, 32–33
  used, 31–32
Ergonomics, 44, 105–6
Errands, 50–52
Essential oils, 89–91
Exercise
  alternatives to, 92
  and biorhythms, 98–99
  personal trainers for, 110
  for repetitive stress injuries,
    105–6, *105, 106*
  time for, 97, 109
Expenses, reimbursable, 136,
    140–41
Experts, hiring
  accountants, 144
  attorneys, 144
  diet and exercise consultants, 110
  equipment consultants, 44
  interior designers/decorators, 24
  organization consultants, 70

  public relations consultants, 128
  travel agents, 128
  writers, 144

F

Family life. *See also* Children
  and interruptions, 62
  separating work from, 47
Fatigue. *See* Revitalization
Fax machines
  buying, 34, 36
  using, 118–19
Fear, 79, 83
Federal ID number, 136
Fees, setting, 138–41
Feng shui, 11
Fictitious name, 114
File cabinets, 7, 38, 43
Files
  current, 29
  security of, 38
  storing, 15
Filing, 55–58
Finances
  collections, 141
  fear about, 79, 83
  income, 138–39
  learning about, 73, 81
  monthly/yearly tasks, 143
  records of, 135–37
  start-up, 74–75, 132–33
Fire extinguishers, 38
Fish tanks, and feng shui, 11
Flexibility
  as personality trait, 82
  in work space design, 18
Floor covering, 10–12
Floor plans, and buying
    equipment, 35
Food supplements, 101

Other Storey Titles You Will Enjoy

Be Your Own Home Decorator, by Pauline G. Guntlow. Explains how to customize kitchens, bedrooms, living rooms, and baths, and shows ways to maximize storage and enhance space. 144 pages. Paperback. ISBN 0-88266-945-1.

Growing Your Own Herb Business, by Bertha Reppert. Includes practical advice on budgets, locations, business plans, bookkeeping, staffing, inventory, and pricing. 144 pages. Paperback. ISBN 0-88266-612-6.

Keeping Fitness Simple, by Porter Shimer. Provides reasons and ways to fit exercise into the reader's life, regardless of time, space, setting, or equipment. 176 pages. Paperback. ISBN 1-58017-034-X.

Keeping Life Simple, by Karen Levine. Offers hundreds of tips for taking positive, effective control of time, money, home, and life. 160 pages. Paperback. ISBN 0-88266-943-5.

Keeping Work Simple, by Don Aslett and Carol Cartaino. Provides tips for simplifying any work environment to achieve maximum job satisfaction and peak performance. 160 pages. Paperback. ISBN 0-88266-996-6.

Too Busy to Clean?, by Patti Barrett. An ingenious collection of simple, clever ways to make cleaning more tolerable and efficient. 160 pages. Paperback. ISBN 1-58017-029-3.

*These books and other Storey books are available
wherever fine books are sold or directly from
Storey Publishing, Schoolhouse Road, Pownal, Vermont 05261,
or by calling 1-800-441-5700. www.storeybooks.com*